IN PRAISE OF *THE COMI*

"For many of us, the world's problems just ⬚⬚⬚⬚⬚⬚⬚⬚⬚⬚⬚⬚
so much easier for us to retreat from them ⬚⬚⬚⬚⬚⬚⬚⬚⬚⬚⬚⬚
Revolution offers raw inspiration and biblica⬚⬚⬚⬚⬚⬚⬚⬚⬚⬚⬚⬚⬚⬚⬚⬚⬚⬚s
to participate in the spiritual and physical tra⬚⬚⬚⬚⬚⬚⬚⬚ation of their world. This book
emanates out of the personal experiences of Dave Donaldson and Convoy of Hope,
who have served nobly in mobilizing hundreds of thousands of people to distrib-
ute vast amounts of resources and live out the whole gospel of Jesus Christ among
the poor and suffering."

RICH STEARNS
president, World Vision

"This book is a clear biblical call for compassion for the poor. Dave Donaldson provides practical guidance and a powerful witness to the transformation God brings
about in everyone involved when we join the compassion revolution."

JONATHAN T.M. RECKFORD
CEO, Habitat for Humanity International

"The convoy of compassionate groups is growing, and Dave Donaldson is playing
a prominent role. *The Compassion Revolution* shows that relational justice—people
helping others, one to one—is the key to developing social justice."

MARVIN OLASKY
editor in chief, *World* magazine
provost, The King's College, New York City

"*The Compassion Revolution* is a passionate and persuasive book that will move you
to tears, cause you to laugh, and inspire you to make a difference."

ANNE BEILER
founder of Auntie Anne's Pretzels

"*The Compassion Revolution* challenges readers to serve the poor and suffering in
America and around the world. I have seen Convoy of Hope grow to help millions
by providing them with food, clean water, and shelter. It has truly been a catalyst
for meeting physical and spiritual needs."

GEORGE O. WOOD
general superintendent, Assemblies of God

"The cross is both vertical and horizontal. It leads to salvation and transformation,
covenant and community, John 3:16 and Matthew 25. In *The Compassion Revolution*,
Dave Donaldson reconciles the vertical and horizontal elements of the Christian

message, mobilizing a movement of hope that will feed the hungry in both body and soul. Let the revolution begin!"

SAMUEL RODRÍGUEZ
president, National Hispanic Christian Leadership Conference

"Dave Donaldson is a gifted leader in the swelling flood of evangelicals and Pentecostals embracing the biblical call to share God's concern for the poor. This book reflects that wonderful development and offers important inspiration and guidance."

RONALD J. SIDER
president, Evangelicals for Social Action
author of *Rich Christians in an Age of Hunger*

"This book will give you an insider's look at compassion ministry and turn your world upside down—or maybe I should say, right side up."

MARK BATTERSON
pastor and bestselling author

"A must read for Christians worldwide. These are the issues we must confront. And this is the legacy of hope we must leave. And all written by a man who has overcome extraordinary challenges to make an extraordinary impact on the world."

DOUG WEAD
former senior advisor for presidents
George H. Bush and George W. Bush

"Dave Donaldson's life is a testament to the transforming force of Christian love and compassion. He loves because he was loved first; he shows compassion because it was first shown to him. *The Compassion Revolution* tells the story of the power of the gospel that must be good news to the poor and freedom for the oppressed. Any true Jesus revolution is always a compassion revolution."

JIM WALLIS
president of Sojourners
author of *The Great Awakening*

"David Donaldson and Convoy of Hope have changed the lives of millions living in poverty as they have responded to God's command to serve 'the least of these.' The National Day of Prayer Task Force has counted it a privilege to lend our support to their work. This book provides an inspiring glimpse of what can result when we minister healing to the poor among us so that our communities can be transformed and mobilized to reach beyond to a suffering world."

JOHN BORNSCHEIN
executive director, National Day of Prayer Task Force

THE COMPASSION REVOLUTION

DAVE DONALDSON
with TERRY GLASPEY

HARVEST HOUSE PUBLISHERS

EUGENE, OREGON

Cover by Left Coast Design, Portland, Oregon

Cover photo © Blue_Cutler / iStockphoto.com

Backcover author photo by Nancy E. Trapp-Chen

THE COMPASSION REVOLUTION
Copyright © 2010 by Dave Donaldson
Published by Harvest House Publishers
Eugene, Oregon 97402
www.harvesthousepublishers.com

Library of Congress Cataloging-in-Publication Data
    Donaldson, Dave.
    The compassion revolution / Dave Donaldson; with Terry Glaspey.
        p. cm.
    ISBN 978-0-7369-2797-0 (pbk.)
    1. Compassion—Religious aspects—Christianity. 2. Suffering—Religious aspects—Christianity. I. Glaspey, Terry W. II. Title.
    BV4647.S9D66 2010
    241'.4—dc22

                                                          2009032070

Printed in the United States of America

10 11 12 13 14 15 16 17 18 / VP-SK / 10 9 8 7 6 5 4 3 2 1

To my mother, Betty—

You turned your wounds into healing for the wounded
You were both a mom and a dad to your fatherless children
You lived an extraordinary life by giving it away
You inspired a compassion revolution

Acknowlegments

Before acknowledging any other person, I want to give God glory for allowing me to share in His compassion revolution and write about it.

This book was made possible because Bob Hawkins, president of Harvest House Publishers, believed in the project and invested the time, talent, and resources of his staff to make it possible. Among Harvest House's quality team is my coauthor, Terry Glaspey, and my editor, Gene Skinner. Partnering with these men has been a joy, and I am thankful for their patience and motivation during this lengthy and rewarding process.

Many of the inspirational stories sprinkled throughout this book are from my work with Convoy of Hope, which has partnered with churches, organizations, businesses, donors, and a vast army of volunteers to touch 30 million people. Here is a sampling of the leaders who have faithfully stood with us: Tom Trask, George Wood, Cardinal Keeler, Glen Cole, Rick Cole, Dick Foth, Jim Bradford, Robert Spence, John Lendal, Mark Batterson, Tommy Sparger, Sam Johnson, George Raduano, Del Tarr, Paul Cedar, Hugh Rosenberg, Brad Rosenberg, Terry Kirk, Larry Hickey, Dan de Leon, Terry Inman, Calev Meyers, Sam Farina, Fred Franks, Mark Lehman, Scott Young, Jesse Miranda, Sam Rodriquez, David and Betty Cribbs, Randy Barton and Bob Clay, Pat Robertson, Michael Little, Terry Meeuwsen, Ron Hembree, and John Damoose.

I cannot adequately express my thanks to Larry Rust, Betty Rath, Bob Reccord, Mike McClaflin, Paul Thompson, Jim Wallis, Pam Pryor, Wendell Vinson, Tom Knox, John Pentz, Doug Wead, and Wendel Cover, who have fanned the flame of compassion within me.

My heart is also filled with gratitude toward God for blessing me with such a wonderful family. This includes my dad and grandmother, who live in heaven, my mom, Betty, and her godly husband, Bernie, and my siblings, Hal, Steve, and Susan. And my better *two-thirds*, Kristy, who (after my salvation) is God's greatest treasure for me. Together we are raising future compassion revolutionaries—our four children, Breahn, Barbara, David, and Brooke.

CONTENTS

FOREWORD

Faith without deeds is dead. Dead! As Christians, we should let this be deeply ingrained in our understanding of what it means to follow Jesus. God's love is expressed to and through us in the care of our neighbor.

But very few of us live up to Jesus' admonition to the rich young ruler and express our love by sacrificially giving to the poor. I did not grow up reading the Bible, but I have made this a practice in our family. I have been struck recently with the force of God's Word to us in this regard, especially through the prophet Isaiah.

"The LORD enters into judgment against the elders and leaders of his people: 'It is you who have ruined my vineyard; the plunder from the poor is in your houses. What do you mean by crushing my people and grinding the faces of the poor?' declares the Lord, the LORD Almighty" (Isaiah 3:14-15). We are all implicated in this passage, not only by what we have done but also by what we have left undone. God is not interested in our empty words or deedless faith.

"Is not this the kind of fasting I have chosen: to loose the chains of injustice and untie the cords of the yoke, to set the oppressed free and break every yoke? Is it not to share your food with the hungry and to provide the poor wanderer with shelter—when you see the naked, to clothe him, and not to turn away from your own flesh and blood?" (Isaiah 58:6-7). Jesus announced

His mandate and mission in Luke 4:18 by quoting Isaiah 61:1-2 and applying it to Himself: "The Spirit of the Lord is on me, because he has anointed me to preach good news to the poor. He has sent me to proclaim freedom for the prisoners and recovery of sight for the blind, to release the oppressed, to proclaim the year of the Lord's favor." And now He sends His disciples, you and me, to go into the world as He was sent into the world.

Dave Donaldson and Convoy of Hope give us a picture of what it means to follow in Jesus' footsteps, preaching the good news to the poor and healing the sick, and they provide a way for us to take action. Although I worked on a paradigm within public policy called "compassionate conservatism," this is a very personal conversation. We are all implicated. We read, we hear, and the question put to us is, how will we respond?

I appreciate the very personal response you will read about in this book. And I appreciate the reminder that we are all part of a body, the bride of Christ, called to be His hands and feet. We all have a part in His mission and ministry to preach the good news, to care for the orphans and widows, and to heal the sick. As you read this book, you will be challenged and equipped. May we not be like the rich young ruler and walk away.

RICK SANTORUM
former United States Senator

PREFACE

When we started Convoy of Hope in 1994, we were surprised by the amount of criticism we received from Christians for feeding the hungry. Some claimed we were leading churches away from their mission of saving souls. In response, we replied, "We're just trying to emulate Jesus. Didn't He go from one village to another, meeting both physical and spiritual needs?" Still, some didn't appreciate our emphasis on helping the poor.

Fortunately, much has changed since 1994. More churches and organizations have dedicated themselves to feeding the hungry, bringing aid to the suffering, and rescuing victims of the sex trade. Convoy of Hope is one of those organizations God has raised up to be a part of the compassion revolution.

As you read this book, invite God to increase your compassion for the poor and suffering. Ask Him to help you become more like Jesus.

HAL DONALDSON

1

ARE YOU READY FOR A REVOLUTION?

magine for a moment that you are relaxing at home and the phone rings. When you answer, you hear a friend's breathless voice: "Are you watching the news? Have you heard what has happened? It's horrible!" Grabbing the remote and turning on the television, you immediately discover that something earthshaking has taken place. Nearly every channel is being interrupted by a special report, so you flip over to your favorite news network.

The news anchor's expression is grim as he announces an unbelievable tragedy. During this one day, 30 jumbo jets have crashed, killing a total of 5700 people. You are transfixed at the enormity of the catastrophe—30 jumbo jets filled with passengers!

Of course, such a tragedy would keep news crews busy for many days and fill the front-page headline in every newspaper. Every news network would lead its broadcast with the story and examine it from every angle. Commentators would analyze what went wrong and how it happened. Public officials and private citizens would pour out their expressions of grief and sorrow for the victims.

Don't you think the whole world would be shocked and in mourning at the announcement of this awful event?

Of course, this didn't happen—these 30 jets didn't crash. But the children who died today simply because they lack clean, safe water would fill *all of these planes*.

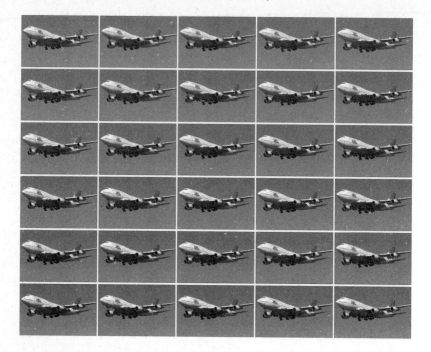

If you add the children who died today because they lack nutritious food, they would fill one of the largest stadiums in America—Michigan Stadium, which has seating capacity for 107,501 fans—twice.

Statistics like these can be overwhelming. The enormity of the problem can loom so large that you feel helpless and hopeless and choose to turn away. Looking into the face of a problem of this size takes guts.

The needs in our world are immense. Throughout this book, we will take an honest look at some of the tragic problems that face our world. And this tragedy is not about abstractions—numbers and graphs and charts. It's about real, living human beings like you and me, people who are struggling against the odds, hoping to find a better life for their sons and daughters, and expending most of their energy just trying to survive. Many of them are fighting a losing battle. Millions in our world, adults and children alike, are without adequate food, without clean water, without even the most rudimentary health care, without housing and shelter, and without much hope for the future.

At the same time, others throughout the world—and you and I are among them—have plenty. While some people have little or no food, we have full pantries and refrigerators. While some have to walk many miles to obtain a jug of clear water, all we have to do is turn the faucet. While children die of treatable diseases and adults go without much-needed medical attention, most of us have ready access to doctors who can deal with even our smallest physical complaints. And while countless people have either no shelter or one that is makeshift at best, we sit in the comfort of our homes—maybe reading a book like this one.

The point of this book is not to make anyone feel guilty, sad, depressed, or angry.

Of course, if we look the problem squarely in the eye, we are likely to have one or more of these responses. But these feelings alone don't do very much to change anything.

The point of this book is to offer hope that something can be done, that much of the suffering abroad and in our own country and our own neighborhood can be alleviated, lessened, or eliminated altogether. We don't have to simply accept that the problems exist and wring our hands over them. We can do something about these problems.

The goal of this book is to offer a vision for how you and I can begin to make changes that will make a difference. We want to look honestly at the problems we face, share inspiring stories about people who are making a difference and about those whose lives have been changed by the help they have received, and offer practical solutions that you and I can be a part of.

The goal of this book is to inspire you to join the compassion revolution.

Jesus, the Revolutionary

A revolutionary is someone who looks at the status quo and says, "This isn't good enough. We can do better." Revolutionaries look at the huge amount of change that is needed, and instead of averting their eyes from the problem, they see opportunity. Revolutionaries feel the stirrings within to stop turning a deaf ear or complaining, and they actually decide to do something about the situation. Revolutionaries join forces with others who have the same concerns so that together, they can make a difference.

A revolution based on compassion is gaining force all around us. Those who are joining this revolution believe that our world can be a better, healthier, safer place for our fellow human beings and that God has called us to His work of bringing health and healing to those in need. We sometimes think of compassion as feeling sorry for people, but that characterization is far too limited. *Compassion* is an action word.

In Luke 6:36, Jesus instructs His followers, "Be merciful, just as your Father is merciful." *Merciful* and *compassionate* are words that describe how we are to *be*, not simply how we are to feel. When we think about Jesus' earthly ministry, we quickly realize that no one has ever modeled compassion the way He did. But think about this—Jesus actually believes that you and I can rise to the standard of being compassionate in the way that God the Father is compassionate. How can that be possible? Could it be that because we are created in the image of God (Genesis 1:27), we carry His compassion DNA? Could we have within us the potential to demonstrate the kind of compassion that Jesus showed throughout His ministry?

At the very beginning of His public work among us, Jesus announced His calling and the nature of His ministry—His mission statement. Quoting the words of the prophet Isaiah, Jesus declared His purpose of reaching out to the outcasts of humanity, those in the deepest need:

> The Spirit of the Lord is on me,
>> because he has anointed me
>> to preach good news to the poor.
> He has sent me to proclaim freedom for the prisoners
>> and recovery of sight for the blind,
> to release the oppressed,
>> to proclaim the year of the Lord's favor (Luke 4:18-19).

Jesus was announcing His intention of practicing a kind of compassion that wasn't just about words, but about actions. Jesus' compassion was revolutionary because it addressed both the spiritual roots and the social consequences of people's problems.

Of course, you might be thinking, *I like to think of myself as a compassionate person who responds with empathy to human suffering, but how can I possibly hope to practice the level of compassion that Jesus demonstrated?* How indeed! He freed people from spiritual bondage and challenged the legalism of the religious authorities. He cared for the sick and the lame, many times choosing to bring miraculous healing. He touched the outcasts of society, both physically and emotionally. He brought the kind of good news that changed everything for people without hope. How could we even think to emulate Jesus' demonstration of power and compassion?

When the disciples posed the same question to Jesus, His response was to raise the bar even higher: "I tell you the truth, anyone who has faith in me will do what I have been doing. He will do even greater things than these, because I am going to the Father" (John 14:12). Surely this is one of the most startling promises in the Scriptures. In John 16:7, Jesus tells us that He is leaving us with the power of the Holy Spirit so we might follow in His footsteps. Through the Spirit, Jesus continues to do His work in and through His people—even people like you and me. God's strength within us empowers us to become compassion revolutionaries.

Can you begin to envision living this kind of revolutionary lifestyle, with Jesus working through you to bring love and hope and healing to others? At its root, that is what being a compassion revolutionary is all about!

2

"YOUR DAD IS IN HEAVEN"
A Convoy of Hope

On an August day in 1969, a local pastor huddled together with me and my brothers. I could tell something was seriously wrong just by the look in his eyes. He nervously glanced back and forth between the three of us, as if trying to find the right words to say and to anticipate whether we would be able to accept them. He cleared his throat and then spoke the brief words that would change my life.

"Your dad is now in heaven," he said.

Nothing had prepared me for this moment, a moment I still remember clearly all these years later.

"Your parents have been in an automobile accident that has killed your father." He searched our faces and found only shock and disbelief. "Your mother was in the car too, and she's in serious condition, but the doctors believe she will live."

At nine years old, I just didn't know how to process this news. People die in movies, but not in real life. And certainly not my dad. "You'll see," I assured my brothers. "In a few hours, they'll be home, and it will all be okay."

The tears flowed freely from my older brother's eyes and fell softly to the pavement as he tried unsuccessfully to be brave for his little brother. His tears rattled my confidence, but I refused to believe that I would not see my father again.

"Where are Mom and Dad?" I pleaded to the pastor. "When are they coming back?"

He gently took my shoulders in his hands, bent down to my level, and looked me squarely in the eyes. "David, your mom is going to be fine, but your dad is now in heaven."

Dad's Second Wind

My father had been a pastor of a small church, working hard to preach the gospel of Jesus and to care for the least and the lost in our community and around the world. He was a man of conviction and compassion whose simple dream of providing a home for his family was cut short when a drunk driver coming in the opposite direction drifted into his lane and collided violently with the car in which my mom and dad were driving. Dad died instantly.

But did his dream of presenting the love of God through acts of compassion die with him? No, God was to have the last word.

Predicting His own death, Jesus said, "I tell you the truth, unless a kernel of wheat falls to the ground and dies, it remains only a single seed. But if it dies, it produces many seeds" (John 12:24). My father's death was the seed that eventually produced Convoy of Hope. My brothers and I (and a host of friends) have carried on a second wind that has multiplied a harvest of hope to every corner of the globe. Nearly 30 million lives have been touched directly through the work of this organization. God took our father's crushed and mangled car and turned it into a fleet of Convoy of Hope trucks that have delivered millions of pounds of emergency supplies to people in need through our disaster relief programs. And in our community outreaches and relief assistance, millions more lives have been touched, bettered, and in many cases, transformed.

Compassion in Action

The nightmare of my parents' accident eventually gave birth to a dream in 1994, when we founded Convoy of Hope with the intention of serving the poor in the United States and around the world. The way we seek to do that is primarily through disaster relief, community outreaches, and international programs. Convoy of Hope mobilizes the army of compassion to be there as quickly as possible with help and supplies when disaster strikes anywhere in the world. We help provide food and clean water to needy communities overseas. And every year we hold dozens of Convoy of Hope outreaches in cities around the United States, setting up in a park or arena or stadium and joining with churches, local charity organizations, and volunteers to provide food, medical care, job placement services, counseling, and spiritual guidance to the needy of that community.

Convoy of Hope World Distribution Center.

From our World Distribution Center in Springfield, Missouri, we extend our efforts from around the block to around the globe. We also have a fleet of 18-wheel trucks (mostly paid for by young people giving to a program called Speed the Light) that can be deployed for disaster relief, as they were for Hurricane Katrina, or to deliver food and services in one of our community outreaches.

We don't do this alone. We have mobilized more than 250,000 volunteers and partnered with more than 5000 churches and organizations to assist families in need. And we have formed strategic partnerships with government, businesses, professional athletes, and nonprofit organizations to expand our services and build community unity. What an awesome privilege to see how much we can do when we work together! President Harry Truman was right: "It is amazing what you can accomplish if you do not care who gets the credit."

A Rough Start

We've had some interesting adventures over the years. Our very first large Convoy of Hope outreach was in Watts, California, where we distributed groceries and Bibles and provided some entertainment. We were partnering in this endeavor with Operation Blessing, the relief organization of the Christian Broadcasting Network, and had more than 200 volunteers from 20 local churches who were eager to serve. To our amazement, more than 4000 needy children and their families showed up for this outreach.

Although this was our first large event, things seemed to be going well. I was standing with Randy Rich, the outreach coordinator and now a vice president at Convoy, who had nothing but praise for how efficiently everything was running. I was just in the process of agreeing with him when the person overseeing the distribution of bags of groceries came running up and shouting, "They're all gone!" At first I thought he meant the groceries, but no, he meant the volunteers. Most of them had disappeared. When I went to check it out, I saw that nobody was at the table to serve the many who had lined up.

Then I noticed that quite a few people in line were wearing yellow T-shirts—the same yellow T-shirts that the volunteers had been given. Evidently, our volunteers wanted to get their share of free groceries as well! With some laughter, some persuasion, and a bit of bribery we sorted things out, and the volunteers returned to their posts.

In the early days of the community events, we always included a program of local talent—singing, rap, drama, and preaching. Each act was given five minutes, and then a local pastor was asked to give a brief message to close the program. But of course, preachers love to preach. Some of them had probably never been in front of such a large audience before, and they took full advantage of the opportunity. Maybe they thought this was their "Billy Graham moment."

On one occasion, following the music, a local pastor stepped behind the microphone and let loose with a torrent of preaching. He had been instructed to give a five-minute message and then offer an opportunity for people to respond. But as he looked over the crowd of 4000 people, he evidently found extra inspiration as five minutes passed, then ten, then fifteen. After thirty minutes of preaching, he was showing no sign of letting up. I moved to where I was sure he could see me and signaled for him to wrap it up. He just ignored me and launched into another sermon. I tried again, this time giving a less polite "cut it off now" sign. Still no response.

I had no other choice, so I went to the sound technician and told him to turn off the microphone. Suddenly the sound went dead. Thinking we had experienced some sort of technical difficulty, the pastor started anxiously tapping the microphone. But when he looked in my direction again and saw my smile, he finally got the message that the show was over. He'd had his fifteen minutes of fame—and then some!

On another occasion, we met a character whom I named Nick the Brick. There was no denying that Nick was a pretty cool guy. He was also extremely muscular. This young man had graduated from Teen Challenge and had aspirations of joining the Power Team, a group of itinerant evangelists who were also body builders. The Power Team was famous for such feats of strength as tearing phone books in half, breaking bricks, and blowing up hot-water bottles like they were balloons. Not your typical evangelists, for sure, but effective at getting people's attention so they could share the gospel with them.

Nick the Brick wanted to add a "power team" element to one of our community outreach events. I couldn't say no. Besides, I was kind of morbidly curious.

Nick took his place in front of the crowd, wearing a thin bandana around his head. He stood in front of a three-foot stack of cement blocks and announced his intention to break them with his head. The crowd went wild, cheering with approval and anticipation.

He centered himself over the bricks, bowed down gently until his forehead just touched the top brick, and then waved his arms up and down to get the crowd cheering. They responded with even louder whoops and shouts, reaching a feverish pitch of excitement. At that moment Nick smashed his forehead into the bricks with all his might. The first and second layers of bricks crumbled under the mighty force. Nick raised up his hands to accept the cheering and adulation. "Nick! Nick! Nick!" the crowd chanted. And then his knees buckled, and he fell backward, lying motionless on the stage.

He was out cold, but the audience thought it was part of the act and kept chanting his name. I knew better, so I went over and helped revive him. When he came to, it took a minute for him to realize what had happened. "C'mon," I said, "let's get you to the van, where you can lay down."

He wouldn't hear of it. The show must go on. He scrambled to his feet, and the audience applauded feverishly.

Still a little concerned, but knowing it was what he wanted, I announced to the crowd, "For his final feat, Nick the Brick will run through two two-by-fours." I took one end of the two pieces of wood, and someone else held the other. Nick counted off 20 paces, inhaled, and stared down the boards like a bull stares down a bullfighter.

Throwing all caution to the wind, he sprinted toward the target as fast as he could, head up and chest out as he smashed into the boards. There was a deafening, splintering crack that echoed through the park where we were holding the event.

As Nick crumbled to the ground, it became obvious that the crack did not come from the boards, but from Nick's ribs. Several guys had to gather up our fallen hero and transport him to the local hospital, where he was treated for a concussion and broken ribs. For him, this was the cost of entertaining the poor. When he recovered, Nick returned as one of the crowd favorites, doing more death-defying stunts. But from that time on, he wore a padded head scarf and omitted the board-breaking stunt from his act.

A Dream Come True!

As you can see, our work includes a lot of fun and adventure—and a little pain. I wouldn't trade anything for these opportunities to serve the poor by meeting practical needs and even providing a little fun.

Over the years, we have responded to disasters and crises in more than 100 countries. We have built shelters, set up water purification units, and provided other necessary supplies to those in need around the globe. We have distributed millions of dollars worth of food to nearly 30 million people. And we have conducted several hundred community outreaches here and abroad. Every year, Convoy of Hope conducts these outreaches in 50 cities and 10 countries.

All in all, it is a big impact. But we don't measure our success by these numbers as much as we do by the stories of individuals whose lives have been impacted through our ministry. That is what really excites us! As you read these pages, you'll find lots of stories about the amazing things God has done through the work of Convoy of Hope and how He has worked in my life. But this book really isn't about Convoy of Hope. It is about you and me and how we can all help make a difference in our damaged and broken world. Many of my stories are set in the work of Convoy of Hope because it is such an important part of my life and the way God has used me. But I'm not trying to sell you on Convoy of Hope. I am trying to help you catch a vision for what you can do in your own life, your own community, your own neighborhood. You may not think that you, one person, can do that much, but we have to start somewhere. "Someone asked Mother Teresa, 'Don't you think what you do is kind of a drop in the bucket?' And she answered, 'No, it's a drop in the ocean. But if I didn't do it, it would be one less drop.'"[1]

The psalmist said, "I know that the LORD secures justice for the poor and upholds the cause of the needy" (Psalm 140:12). Doing compassion work is like slipping into Jesus' sandals and doing His work. In this book, I'd like to challenge you to think about a new way of living in which compassion for others is a priority that leads to caring, giving, and serving people with needs.

Let's join the compassion revolution!

3

WITH

Welcome. You are with family, and this is now your home."

These words, spoken by a member of Dad's church, marked the beginning of the long process of healing following my father's death. That one little four-letter word *with* transformed the lives of what remained of our family.

I often lay awake in the dark on many nights following that tragic day, wondering what would happen to us next, where we would live, and who would watch over us. I worried that I would be separated from my siblings. After all, who would be willing to take in four children? We moved around for a number of days, and with each stop, I wondered if this would finally be the place where we would settle.

My grandmother assured us, "God is a Father to the fatherless, and He is watching over you."

"How can God be our Father when He's all the way up in heaven?" I asked.

"Just watch," she said, "He will fulfill His promise through His people." And He did.

The night I heard the words that opened this chapter, I followed a stone path to a trailer owned by the Davis family. The Davises were faithful members of my dad's congregation. Bill Davis ran the Sunday school, and his wife, Louvada, directed the women's ministry. The Davises didn't have a lot of money. They lived in a trailer with their two children, and we had often visited them there. But walking up the path with my suitcase in one hand and my pillow clutched in the other, I knew this was unlike any previous visit. For now, weary from weeks of being fatherless and homeless and from moving about from house to house, we were going to settle down in a new place.

The Davises' mobile home, where ten of us lived.

I worried that they were reaching out to us only out of a sense of duty, and I thought to myself that they probably didn't really want us there. But when I reached up to knock on the door, it swung open, and Mr. Davis was there, standing in the threshold with a warm, inviting smile.

As we shuffled inside, Mr. Davis embraced each of us and spoke those life-changing words: "Welcome. You are with family, and this is now your home."

That little word *with* meant that the Davis family was sharing more than their home with us. They also shared in our loss and pain. I felt the cold loneliness lift off my shoulders as I was embraced by the Davis family's love. God was using them to fulfill His promise.

LOUVADA REMEMBERS...

When we invited the Donaldsons into our mobile home, it got crowded at times, but by God's grace we all made it through. Our home had three bedrooms, and two of them were only seven feet by eight feet. Counting my family, we had six children and four adults—a total of ten people occupying a mobile home. The Donaldsons' grandmother slept in one room, and Dave's sister, Susan, stayed with my daughter, who had bunk beds. Betty Donaldson joined us after a long stay in the hospital and slept in our living room. We had to eat in shifts because our dining area could accommodate only four people. We had only one bathroom, so I assigned the six kids specific times in the morning to get ready for school. As I reflect back, I do not remember it being hard. We were family and still are.

God demonstrates His compassion toward us by entering into the human condition and feeling our pain and anguish, our spiritual and physical impoverishment, our hopelessness and fear. Jesus is called Immanuel for that very reason. Immanuel means "God with us" (Matthew 1:23). This is the very heart of the compassion revolution. God, the Creator of the universe, entered our pain to bring help, healing, and hope. So we too, as His followers, should enter into other people's pain to bring them practical help and a connection to Him who is the source of all hope.

Jesus in the Mud

We held a Convoy of Hope outreach in Baltimore in a grassy field that turned into a muddy swamp after days of torrential rain. But these sloppy conditions and rain could not dampen the enthusiasm of the 1000 volunteers who had prepared to serve the multitude of needy people with groceries, haircuts, job résumés, and activities for the kids. One volunteer swept by me in her bare feet with mud thigh-high on her jeans and oozing between her toes. She laughed, "This is like Woodstock for the poor!"

And so it was. A joyful and messy celebration of caring and compassion.

Later that day, I gave a tour of the outreach site to Lenny Moore, who played for the Baltimore Colts and is now a member of the NFL Hall of Fame and a representative for the NFL-sanctioned Courage Awards Foundation. Lenny had made the mistake of wearing white tennis shoes. Before long, his shoes and pants were covered in mud. He joked that it reminded him of some of the games he used to play on muddy fields.

As we walked through the Kids Zone, the area set off for activities for children, a woman recognized Lenny and pointed him out to others nearby. "Look!" she exclaimed, "there's Lenny Moore, the famous football player!" She hurried over to meet Lenny and shake his hand.

"I can't believe you would be out here with us in the mud!" she said with amazement and disbelief. But that is what compassion is all about: being with those in need.

Lenny could have stayed in his clean, dry, comfortable home. But instead, he and a thousand other volunteers had chosen to venture out into a muddy field to be with these less fortunate members of the community.

Of course, this is just like what Jesus did for us. He left the glory of heaven to live with us in the mud and pain and darkness of the human condition in order to cleanse us from our messiness and sin. And much of His ministry was focused on the muddiest people in the muddiest places. He was never afraid to go where the need was greatest, regardless of how much it cost. The apostle Paul challenges us to follow Him there:

> Your attitude should be the same as that of Christ Jesus:
> Who, being in very nature God,
>> did not consider equality with God as something
>>> to be grasped,
> but made himself nothing,
>> taking the very nature of a servant,
>> being made in human likeness.
> And being found in appearance as a man,
>> he humbled himself
>> and became obedient to death—
>> even death on a cross! (Philippians 2:5-7).

This passage captures the countercultural, counterintuitive nature of how God came to us in Jesus Christ. As theologian Karl Barth so vividly described it, "From the heights to the depth, from victory to defeat, from riches to poverty, from triumph to suffering, from life to death." Jesus, who could probably have simply "fixed things" from on high, chose a different path. He became a servant to humanity. He became one of us and entered fully into our experience.

The mystery of God's love is not that He takes away our pain, but that He is willing to share in our suffering. In our moments of loneliness and anguish, God is with us.

To Suffer With

The word *compassion* means "to suffer with." If we choose to exercise compassion, we will undoubtedly get messy and muddy as we come alongside others and experience some of their pain and suffering. When the automobile accident took my father's life and broke my mother's body, our lives became muddy and messy. My brothers and I were emotional wrecks and had many needs. If the Davis family had visited my mother in the hospital and perhaps offered us food, clothing, and money, they would have been admired for their caring. Those actions would have been wonderful. But they did more than that. They fully embraced our troubles, sadness, confusion, and anger by inviting us into their home and into their lives. They became compassion incarnate by being fully *with* us.

Several times the Gospels reveal that Jesus was moved by compassion. The Greek word used in the original texts (*splangchna*) speaks of something happening deep inside us—in our intestines, our guts. It is a word of inner upheaval and violence. When Jesus saw needs, He did not simply feel a nice tidy bit of pity. No, He felt an internal churning of deepest sympathy and compassion. He became sick with the sick, grief-stricken with the grieving, and hurt for the hurting.

Some of these for whom Jesus was moved by such compassion were victims. Life had taken its toll on them. They were orphaned, widowed, disabled, or the recipients of neglect and abuse. What happens within us when we see children whose stomachs are bloated because of malnutrition? When we see single parents working hard but still not making enough to sustain their children? When we are shown photos of hopeless children in orphanages or widows who sit alone and neglected in squalid apartments? We quickly feel a deep and moving compassion for these people.

But what about those who seem to have brought their problems upon themselves or who appear to be manipulating the system to get help? Do we feel compassion toward the single mom who is milking the programs to garner more public funds? Are we moved when we see homeless people who have been hollowed out by drug addiction? Is there any compassion for the prisoner who has committed a heinous crime and now wastes away behind bars?

Don't we sometimes practice a selective compassion, differentiating between those we deem deserving of it and those we don't? But think about Jesus. Did He feel less compassion for those whose own bad choices had brought them to a place of need? Are we not all sinners in need of a Savior? Doesn't the well-known phrase "There but for the grace of God go I" really apply to all of us? Jesus, the original compassion revolutionary, sees these people and their own unique struggles, and He is moved to compassion. They are His creation, His children, objects of His mission. "For the Son of Man came to seek and to save what was lost" (Luke 19:10).

In the ultimate demonstration of compassion, Jesus looked down from the cross and saw the very people who put Him there—the ones who betrayed Him, spat upon Him, and whipped His body into splinters of flesh. He gazed down upon a group of people, not a single one of them truly and fully innocent, and prayed, "Father, forgive them, for they do not know what they are doing" (Luke 23:34).

A Prisoner of Hope

As I write this chapter, I am looking out my hotel window into the busy streets of Beijing, China. This is my second visit to China, and much has changed during the past 15 years. Religious persecution still exists, but the freedom to practice the Christian faith is emerging. Not long ago, though, to do so was to risk incarceration.

During my last visit, I learned the story of a young woman who was having a profoundly effective ministry in preaching the gospel. Thousands were leaving their other religious beliefs and accepting Jesus Christ as their Lord and Savior. Since preaching the gospel or engaging in any kind of pros-elytizing was illegal, she was finally arrested and taken to a high-security prison dominated by male prisoners.

The guards beat her as fellow prisoners cheered. They put her in a cell that was dark and cold and did not even include a toilet. One would think that her attitude would have been anger toward God and resentment toward her guards and fellow prisoners. But in the depth of her faith, she had developed compassion like that of Jesus. She prayed, "God, I am unsure why You have placed me here, but it must be for Your glory. Please show me how to reach this prison for You."

One of the reasons the guards were so angry at the prisoners was that with no toilets in the cells, when they delivered the prisoners' meager food, they also had to come into the cells and scoop up their excrement. One day, shortly after she prayed that prayer, the guard came by to perform his usual unpleasant duty. She said to him, "A guard should not have to clean up a prisoner's waste; that's a job for a prisoner."

The guard thought for a moment and then replied, "You're right. Here is the shovel and pail—now go clean out every cell."

Following orders, she went from cell to cell, scooping up the human waste. It became her regular duty, and she did it without complaining. But the guard did not realize that as she visited each cell, she brought a kindly greeting and the good news of the gospel. She shared the story of Jesus with each prisoner, and before long most of them had received Jesus as their Savior. Then these newly converted prisoners began witnessing to the guards and even the warden. The entire prison was eventually transformed by the power of the message of Jesus—and by a servant's heart of compassion.

This young woman was a compassion revolutionary who believed that Jesus can change hearts and change the world. She saw in her captors and fellow prisoners something deeper than their actions. She saw that they suffered from the deepest captivity—that of sin and separation from God. And she found a way—not a pleasant way, but a powerful and creative way—to truly be *with* her prison mates.

The Power of *With*

The principle of *with* can change the way we see social problems and view the poor. The labels we use to describe them are often well-meaning and probably sometimes unavoidable, but they fail to adequately express how God sees people with needs. When I hear the phrase "the less fortunate," I always am brought up short by the implication "My fate is better than your fate." Or the differentiation between the "haves" and the "have-nots." This kind of language seems to draw a distinction and create a separation between "us" and "them." That kind of distinction just isn't helpful, and it is not the way Jesus sees all of us. To Jesus, helping the poor is not...

> bending toward the underprivileged from a privileged position; it is not a reaching out from on high to those who are less fortunate below; it's not a gesture of sympathy or pity for those who fail to make it in the upward pull. On the contrary, compassion means going directly to those people and places where suffering is most acute and building a home there.[1]

Whether literally or metaphorically, we need to build a home among the needy, to be among them, to be with them.

We are all loved and valued by God. We all deserve dignity and respect, not just pity and sympathy. The hand that feeds and the hand that receives are both hands held by God, knitted together for His purposes, co-laborers in His work of demonstrating the glory and justice of God's kingdom. As the apostle Paul reminds us, "There is neither Jew nor Greek, slave nor free, male nor female, for you are all one in Christ Jesus" (Galatians 3:28).

The compassion revolution will sometimes call us to leave our security and safety and venture into uncertainty and discomfort as we follow God's call. I think of Abraham, who left the security of his home in Ur to journey to the land of Canaan. Reflecting on what Abraham was called to do, Hebrews 11:8 tells us, "By faith Abraham, when called to go to a place he would later receive as an inheritance, obeyed and went, even though he did not know where he was going." When Abraham received the call, he did not receive elaborate instructions or directions. He did not know where he was going, but that was not as important as knowing whom he was following.

Throughout the Scriptures we see others who had to step out in faith and obedience, often giving up much of their comfort and security, in order to do God's work of helping others. We see this pattern throughout history as well. Martin Luther left the monastery to take up the dangerous task of speaking against religious abuses and teaching the extent of God's grace and mercy. Dietrich Bonhoeffer, who had fled Nazi Germany to the safety of the United States, was compelled to return to comfort and strengthen his countrymen, even though his decision eventually led to imprisonment and death. Rosa Parks vacated her safe place in the back of the bus to sit with white people in the front, thereby declaring equality and the need for justice.

For these and other revolutionary followers of God, *with* included a physical relocation. The *with* to which God is calling you and me may not always require a major geographical change, but it may well require a change of attitude and a new way of seeing.

It also means a new way of hearing. Our word *obedience* is derived from the Latin word *audiere*, which means "to listen." Our revolutionary work of compassion begins with listening to God and then doing what He asks of us regardless of how radical or uncomfortable it might be. But wherever He calls us or whatever He calls us to do, He will surely be opening the door to an adventure—the adventure of *with*.

With as a Lifestyle

With can become a new way of living—becoming willing to take risks and step outside what we are used to.

When we know people are hurting or grieving, we may feel awkward because we don't know what to say. We may doubt that we could really be of any help. We may even excuse ourselves by thinking, *They probably just want to be left alone.*

When we see poverty and misfortune, we are tempted to turn away and pretend we don't notice. We may justify our inaction: "We already gave at the office," or "I help the poor through paying my taxes—isn't that what my tax dollars are for?" Or we may be moved to write a check and send it off to a good organization, which makes us feel as if we have done all we can do.

But God expects more than that of us. He wants us to enter into the spirit of *with*, to enter into the needs of our friends and of those we don't even know yet.

The apostle Peter reminds us of one of the keystones of Christian living: "Clothe yourselves with humility toward one another" (1 Peter 5:5). Don't picture the kind of clothing you can put on or take off. Rather, it's like skin— permanent, a part of us. We are called to a lifestyle of becoming increasingly others-centered. It is a new way of thinking, of seeing, of believing. Then, when we meet people in pain, there is no question in our mind. We care. We serve. We love. We put their needs above our comfort or convenience. Servanthood becomes a circle of serving others and being served.

WHAT CAN I DO? SOME PRACTICAL WAYS TO MAKE A DIFFERENCE...

- Be *with* a family member or friend who is grieving the loss of a loved one.

- Call or write an encouraging note to someone who lost a job.

- Take a gift to a shut-in's home or retirement center.

- Sit with a person who is sick in the hospital or visit the family.

- Visit a person incarcerated in your local jail or in a prison.

For my family, compassion came full circle when my wife and I felt the Lord nudge us to open our home to foster children. We completed the necessary training and became certified by the state of Virginia to be foster care providers. Before long, a local agency called about a young woman who needed a home.

Our first response was to say no, as we had already decided that we wanted to provide care for a boy. (We already had two girls of our own.) But the woman from the agency wouldn't accept a quick no. "You are the only licensed provider in her school district."

When we heard that, we knew we couldn't respond so quickly, so we made arrangements for her to come to our home for dinner. Almost immediately our hearts were knit together with this lovely teenage girl. We knew this was God's plan for us. It wasn't what we had planned or what we had signed up for, but it was clearly what He wanted.

Days later I remember looking out the front window and watching for the young lady's arrival. After she was dropped off, we watched her approach the house, clearly a little nervous and apprehensive. With one hand she towed along the suitcase filled with her possessions, and with the other she clutched a pillow.

My eyes filled with tears as I reflected back to the day when I walked up the stony path to the Davis home. Just like this young woman now, I had come in search of security and love and a place to call home. Almost 40 years later, here I was, blessed with a wonderful family and living in a nice home. As a leader in Convoy of Hope, I had been part of helping millions of people around the world. But this was personal, a new and deeper step into a lifestyle of *with*.

As the young lady reached the door, I swung it open and stood before her with a warm and inviting smile and tears in my eyes. As she stepped across the threshold, I gave her a hug and said, "Welcome. You are with family, and this is now your home."

4

DO YOU KNOW
MY NAME?

I want to challenge you this week to look for opportunities to reach out and touch the untouchables."

With those words I brought my sermon to a close. The parishioners nodded their heads in agreement, and a sprinkling of amens echoed through the crowd. I always enjoyed challenging and inspiring folks, motivating them to step out of the pews and become involved in compassion ministries, so here I was again, guest preaching at a large church, sharing my heart and the story of Convoy of Hope.

While the pastor began the closing prayer, I did what I usually do. I slipped down the aisle so I could station myself at the doors of the foyer and greet people as they exited the auditorium. In my haste I walked right past a little cluster of homeless men who had come in off the street to participate in the service. They had taken seats in the very back so as to be less conspicuous. I didn't pay much attention to them as I positioned myself to shake hands and smile and answer questions.

As the pastor's prayer continued, the restroom door suddenly opened behind me, and a homeless man shuffled out into the foyer. He looked ragged and dirty, and quite honestly, he didn't smell very good. I glanced in his direction and then back toward the front of the church.

"Do you know my name?"

I turned again, wondering whom he was speaking to. When our eyes met, I saw that he was talking to me. He approached me and repeated his question. "Do you know my name?"

He stood before me with searching eyes.

"I'm sorry, but I don't know your name," I told him.

"My name," he said firmly and with a hint of pride, "is Joe."

"And my name is Dave," I said. We exchanged smiles.

"Do you know why I come here?" he asked. Before I could reply he provided the answer to his own question. "I come here so people will know my name."

It's Personal

For many Americans, the poor are less than fully human figures whom we take care to avoid as we go to the office, or they are sad images that stare out from our television screen. Or maybe they are numbers in a list of troubling statistics we hear quoted. But so often we don't really think of them as persons—people just like you and me.

Jesus never made that mistake about the poor. He looked them in the eye and accepted them as much-loved children of the heavenly Father. When Jesus said, "The poor you will always have with you" (Matthew 26:11), He was saying three very significant things.

First, we will always have the poor among us. It is a concession to the truth that our world will always include people who lack the basic necessities of life.

Second, by saying the poor are always *with* us, Jesus assumes we have a relationship with the poor.

And third, we are left with the responsibility of doing something about their condition.

In the parable of the sheep and the goats, Jesus speaks of helping those without food, water, clothing, and shelter, and He says, "Whatever you did for one of the least of these brothers of mine, you did for me" (Matthew 25:40). As Jesus unfolds this story, He consistently uses personal pronouns—*you*, *my*, and *me*. To Jesus, poverty is personal and relational. Perhaps that is why many people feel closest to Jesus when they are reaching out to help the poor. As Mother Teresa reminds us, Jesus comes to us in the "distressing disguise" of the poor.

To Jesus, poverty always has a face and a name, and behind it are people of unfathomable value. So I must ask myself, do I even know anyone who is poor? If not, what can I do to build a relationship with the poor?

Poverty has a face and a name.

We Didn't Know

We were holding a community outreach on an uncharacteristically sunny day in Minneapolis. We had recruited about a hundred teenagers from local youth groups to assist with serving hot dogs and drinks to the poor who had come for the various services we were offering. As I made the rounds and returned to the spot where the food was being served, I noticed that a bunch of the young people were missing.

"Where did the young volunteers go?" I asked a local coordinator. She shook her head and said, "I don't know. They were here a few minutes ago, and then a bunch of them just disappeared."

I felt some frustration and wondered where they had gone. *Why did they even volunteer if they were just going to slack off?* We needed their help, so I thought I'd better see if I could find them. I strolled around the grounds, asking a number of people if they had seen the young people who were serving hot dogs. No one seemed to know what had happened to them.

About the time I was starting to get a little anxious, I heard some muffled sounds from behind a storage shed. Suspicious, I drew close and heard what sounded like crying. As I rounded the back of the shed, I realized I had found what I was looking for: A huddle of young people were weeping and trying to console one another.

"What's going on?" I gently questioned.

One young woman with smeared makeup, red eyes, and quivering lips spoke up in a sobbing tone. "We didn't know. We didn't know."

"You didn't know what?" I asked.

"We didn't know the poor in our city were families with children."

The other kids chimed in. "We didn't know…We didn't know."

Misconceptions That Separate Us

We so often tend to think of the poor as homeless men who are lazy, on drugs, and feeding off society. We may use soft words, but our thoughts can be harsh: *They made their bed; let them sleep in it.* We blame the poor for their poverty. And we harbor a lot of misconceptions about who the poor really are. Here are some of the generalizations many of us believe.

The poor are lazy. Of course, some people don't have anything to eat because they are unwilling to work. For one reason or another, they have decided that society owes them a living, and they see no reason to expend their energy to find and hold a job. But the truth is that the greatest majority of the poor would love to have a job but cannot find adequate employment because of physical limitations, lack of training, mental problems, or simply the lack of jobs available.

The poor are dangerous. We have all heard stories—some of them nothing more than urban myths—about crazy homeless men who are looking for opportunities to rob and steal and rape. But when you personally get to know the poor, you learn that the percentage of dangerous people among them is just about the same as it is among the rest of the population. The majority of the poor are kind and thoughtful and appreciative and imperfect, just like you and me.

The poor just milk the welfare system. Without question, our government-run programs to assist the poor have problems with loopholes, inequities, nonsensical regulations, and whatnot. Sometimes, therefore, the problem is not with the individual recipients, but with the system itself. I can assure you that most poor people would jump at the chance to work at a decent job instead of enduring the hassles and indignities of the welfare system.

The poor make bad parents. Sometimes we hear stories about parents who abuse and emotionally damage their children because their poverty has driven them beyond what they can handle. But more common are the heroic stories about impoverished parents who will do anything they can—including going without food themselves and making other huge sacrifices—to build a better future for their children. And many of them are more involved in the lives of their kids than are those parents who raise their children in comfortable materialistic neglect because they are so tied up with their own careers and goals.

The poor are just in the big cities. The images of poverty we see on television are mostly from the cities, probably because in them we find a lot of the poor massed together in denser distribution. But throughout the U.S. and the world, many of the most desperately poor live in rural areas, often where there are fewer services and programs available to alleviate their problems.

My brother Steve tells the story of a relief organization in rural Arkansas that delivered a care package to a family of seven living in a mobile home. When the family opened the care package and began to lay the items it contained out on the kitchen table, one of the little girls in the family reached for one of the toothbrushes. She began to weep silently, the tears making rivulets down her smudged cheeks. The relief worker was concerned. "Is something wrong? Is it the wrong color?"

The little girl disappeared for a few moments and returned clutching the new toothbrush to her chest but holding out a very old toothbrush that had been worn down to the nubs. "We have all been using this one," she said.

Unhelpful generalizations and misconceptions often keep us from reaching out. But when we begin to actually get to know poor people—experiencing them as real people, not stereotypes—our attitude begins to change.

My coauthor told me about his experience of working at a temporary homeless shelter at his church. During the winter months, local churches took turns using their sanctuaries or Sunday school classrooms to provide shelter for needy individuals and families. It was a good use of well-heated buildings that are often vacant most days of the week. He told me that he was kind of nervous about volunteering to help, especially when he got his job assignment—just talk with people, be friendly, and make them feel at home. He admitted that he would have felt more at ease cooking for them, washing dishes, or passing out supplies. But instead he spent a few hours just talking—about their families, about some hobbies and interests he shared with them, and about the unfortunate circumstances that had left them in need. He realized how much they were like him. They had just experienced some misfortune that had led them to a different economic destination.

After that evening of truly enjoyable and very normal conversations with these folks, he said he could never think of poor people in the same way again. Now he knew some of their names.

Believing in People

From almost the very beginning of Convoy of Hope we have emphasized the "guest of honor" principle. Each person who attends an outreach is treated as a VIP. Volunteers are instructed not to wear sunglasses so they can make eye contact with our guests and take a personal interest in them. At the outreaches I enjoy greeting the guests as they wait to enter the outreach site. I am always moved by their stories of hardship and perseverance.

Hours before an outreach event in Washington DC, nearly 10,000 people had formed a line around RFK Stadium, where the Washington Redskins play. Since a wind and rain storm had destroyed much of what we had set up in preparation for the event, we had volunteers working feverishly to get things rebuilt and reorganized. This meant that everyone had to wait a little longer than usual. I joined several other volunteers "working the line," encouraging people to wait just a little longer and making sure everyone felt welcomed and properly greeted.

Suddenly, a woman named Louise demanded my attention. "Sir, can you come over here?" Even at a distance I could see that she was annoyed and upset, looking for somewhere to displace her anger. "We have been waiting here patiently, and people keep cutting in front of us," she lamented.

"I'll see what I can do," I said, and I called another volunteer over to talk with her.

Ten minutes later, as I walked back by, I heard her voice again. "Sir, they still taking cuts!" Her face reflected her painful loss of dignity and self-esteem. I tried to think about how I should handle this delicate situation and came up with the best solution I could muster on the spur of the moment.

I asked the woman to step out of the line so that I could speak to her privately. She seemed a bit apprehensive, but she obliged me. "You seem like a responsible person and tough enough to handle these cutters," I said. "Would you be willing to manage this part of the line?"

She stared at me in disbelief as I handed her an event badge. "Do you mean I can be a worker and help you?"

"Yes, Louise, I believe you are the best person to control this line and make sure nobody takes cuts."

As she pinned the badge on her blouse, I saw the expression on her face change from sour to sweet and from frustration to determination. As I walked away I heard her barking out orders to the guests: "We're glad you're here, but understand this—nobody cuts into my line!"

The next time I saw Louise, she was standing alongside the other volunteers at our post-event rally. "Thanks for helping out today, Louise."

She looked at me with a little grimace of a smile and said, "I am tired, but this is the best tired I have been for a long time. When can we do it again?"

WHAT CAN I DO? SOME PRACTICAL WAYS TO MAKE A DIFFERENCE...

- Think honestly and carefully about this question: Do you have any misconceptions about the poor that you need to change?
- Set a goal of building a relationship with at least one person or family that is poor.
- Take the time to talk with a homeless person.
- Volunteer to serve at a homeless shelter.

He Knows My Name

I am amazed every time I see the power of personal contact and the change that happens when we let people know we not only value them but also believe in them. If we could fully grasp the value God places on each person, we would be filled with His love, and it would spill over to touch others. How many people cross our paths who need to know they are the apple of God's eye (Psalm 17:8) and that "even the very hairs of [their] head are all numbered" (Matthew 10:30)?

I joined a crowd in applauding and wiping away tears as the beautiful children of ChildHelp USA descended the platform stairs after performing at the NFL-sanctioned Ed Block Courage Awards banquet. These young singers were at ChildHelp because they had been victims of abuse, and now they were standing before us. The well-to-do crowd could not escape the reality of the visible emotional and physical damage that these innocent young lives had suffered. I thought to myself, *If anyone has a right to be angry and bitter, these kids do.* Yet these bruised and scarred children had just sung with power and conviction the praise song "He Knows My Name."

WHO ARE THE POOR?

As long as we hold on to our misconceptions about the poor, we will be shielded from the truth about the extent of poverty and whom it really affects. We need to realize that a large percentage of the poor is made up of the two most vulnerable groups—the elderly and children.

Aging with Dignity

In the United States, some of the most common victims of poverty are the elderly. These are men and women who worked hard all their lives but were never able to amass a significant nest egg for their future. Sometimes what little they had saved is quickly exhausted in a major medical emergency or some other unforeseen expense, and they find themselves in the category of the needy. Among them are veterans who sacrificed a great deal while fighting for their country in World War II, Korea, or Vietnam. Many are men and women who went without some of the things they wanted so their children could have comfort and safety and a good education to help them get ahead. But now, in their latter years, they find themselves broke and without any means to help themselves.

They depend on their Social Security benefits, which are not really adequate to make ends meet. And so they are left in need—and this is just wrong. They shouldn't have to worry about their medical insurance paying for their surgery, treatments, or prescription drugs. They shouldn't have to stress about what they will do if their home needs repair or a major appliance breaks down. They shouldn't have to worry about being shuffled off to a substandard nursing facility because they can't afford decent care for the final years of their lives.

Currently, 3.5 million Americans age 65 and older live below the poverty line. Millions more barely make ends meet.

> Aging Americans are feeling the effects of the declining real estate and stock markets, as well as soaring fuel and food prices…The nation's health and social services resources will face unprecedented demand as 75 million people in the baby boomer generation reach retirement age—some with eroded savings and retirement accounts.[1]

Former vice president Hubert Humphrey reminded us of our responsibility to our forebears:

> It was once said that the moral test of government is how that government treats those who are in the dawn of life, the children; those who are in the twilight of life, the elderly; and those who are in the shadows of life, the sick, the needy, and the handicapped.

Of these groups, the elderly are most often forgotten, sometimes to die alone and neglected. They once served and waited on us, but now we sometimes discriminate against them.

On a visit to a doctor's office for a routine checkup, I sat down next to a kind elderly couple and struck up a conversation. They looked tired, so I asked them how long they had been waiting. "Oh, about two hours," they told me.

Not long after, the front desk clerk called my name. As I approached the desk, I said, "That couple over there has been waiting for two hours, and I have only been here for about thirty minutes. Why am I getting to go ahead of them even though they have waited so much longer?"

She glanced in their direction and gave me a knowing smile, "Don't worry about it. They have time."

"If you don't have time for them," I said, "then I don't have time for this office." I turned, walked out, and never returned.

Our society sometimes seems to operate on the proposition that if you are not of value to me, then you are expendable. Until we begin to appreciate the legacy a previous generation has left to us and accept responsibility to make sure its members receive good care and are treated with dignity, we have failed to be the kind of society we should be.

Children in America's War Zone

The elderly are not the only vulnerable ones who get overlooked. Sadly, both here and abroad, children are perhaps the greatest victims of poverty and economic injustice. The scourge of the AIDS epidemic has left tens of millions of children as orphans as the disease continues to decimate the adult population in some parts of the world, such as Africa. Estimates are that approximately 210,000 children die every week from lack of food and clean water. Closer to home, millions of kids are growing up in impoverished households, often without exposure to basic values like marital fidelity, drug-free living, and a strong work ethic.

Children who are raised in an environment of dysfunction and poverty often develop a dangerous mix of anger and antisocial behavior. One inner-city pastor told me, "If we are lucky, we have these kids [in our programs] for two or three hours a week. It sometimes feels like taking a tiger out of the jungle for a couple of hours and trying to domesticate it, only to release it back to the jungle." Families who try to raise their children with strong values are up against a real struggle.

> Many people in the inner city strive to follow the so-called decent path. But their ability to challenge street culture is limited. They are under siege, threatened by drug dealers, gangbangers, and addicts, and surrounded by a disproportionate number of chronically unemployed or underemployed, school dropouts, pregnant teens, single-parent households, and families fully dependent on public assistance.[2]

Or consider this haunting description of life in a Chicago housing project:

> Gang rivalries, shootings, drug dealing, and bloodshed make the area a virtual combat zone. Many of the residents do not allow their children to play outside. Instead they crowd all the furniture against one wall in the living room to give the children a play area.[3]

Jonathan Kozol, in his book *Amazing Grace*, describes classrooms in south Bronx where children are given special instructions on what to do when they hear shooting. The classroom walls are pocked with bullet holes.

Beyond financial and educational programs, these children need role models to teach them—up close and personal—a better way to get by in the world and the skills they need to make a better future for themselves.

Somebody Else Will Do It

I never want to romanticize the idea of working with the poor. Yes, they are often kind and appreciative and grateful for the help they are given. But not always. Sometimes they can be rude, unappreciative, and mean.

Let's face it. Rich or poor, some people are easier to love than others. Some light up the room when they enter it; others light up the room by leaving! One of my favorite stories is about a little girl named Suzie who was sitting in her second-grade Sunday school class when the teacher instructed the students, "Raise your hand if you want to go to heaven."

All the students raised their hands but Suzie. Hers remained stubbornly at her side.

"Suzie," the puzzled teacher asked, "don't you want to go to heaven?"

Suzie nodded her head, as if in agreement, but then glanced around the room. "Yes, I want to go to heaven—but not with this bunch!"

I suppose we all feel like Suzie sometimes. But we don't necessarily get to choose the people we serve and help. Sometimes they will be very unlike us. We might not feel entirely comfortable or secure around them. Sometimes they may even be hard and unkind and lack appreciation for what we do. But surely the one who calls us to love our enemies doesn't think a little discomfort is a good excuse not to reach out.

When we look into the faces of the poor, we realize that the problem is personal, not just societal. These are real people with real problems. We can't just assume that a government program is going to do the trick or that somebody else or someone else's church will step in to solve the problems. The belief that somebody else will act (and therefore we don't have to) only perpetuates the problem and keeps it growing.

A television show performed a little experiment. An actor dressed as a businessman walked down the street of a major American city and suddenly collapsed right in the pathway of other walkers. The show's producers wanted to see how long he would lay there before someone helped. As the camera rolled, person after person walked by, at most giving a curious glance at the man who had collapsed on the sidewalk. Fifteen minutes passed, and then 30. Finally, after 45 minutes a fellow citizen stopped, stooped down...and stole his watch.

WHAT CAN I DO? SOME PRACTICAL WAYS TO MAKE A DIFFERENCE...

- Join a Big Brother or Big Sister program for troubled youth.
- Volunteer as a teaching assistant at a local school.
- Organize a prayer walk for your community.

In his book *The Tipping Point*, Malcolm Gladwell writes of experiments on "the bystander problem," trying to determine which situations would get bystanders to help out someone in need. In one experiment, a student alone in his dorm room staged an epileptic fit. The results were interesting. "When there was just one person next door, listening, that person rushed to the student's aid 85 percent of the time. But when subjects thought that there were four others also overhearing the seizure, they came to the student's aid only 31 percent of the time."[4] In other words, if people see others around them, they will assume that someone else is handling the problem and not get involved.

This hit close to home for me one day when I saw a pillar of smoke stretching toward the sky. It was only a few blocks away, so I ran over to see what was happening. Smoke was billowing out of the windows of a burning building. Looking around, I noticed several other neighbors watching the spectacle unfold. Approaching a couple standing across the street, I asked, "Has anyone called the fire department?"

Folding their arms they replied, "Not sure. We assume so."

"Well," I asked, "can I use your phone to make sure?" They agreed, and so I dialed 911. After the emergency operator got the information about the fire and where it was located, I told her that I assumed someone had already reported it, but just wanted to make sure. "No," she said, "you are the first to call."

Then I started wondering if there might be anyone still in the burning building. I imagine all the onlookers assumed that there wasn't...until a woman emerged with a child in each hand. Now the "good neighbors" finally responded and got them out of harm's way. Moments later the fire engines arrived.

This experience taught me a valuable lesson: Never assume anything! It is a motto that has proven to be helpful and important time and again when helping the needy. We are so quick to assume that someone else will step in to help, someone else will reach out his or her hand, and someone else will meet the needs. But when we realize the poor have faces and they are people just like us, we will quit standing still like dazed bystanders and start doing what we can to help.

We are our brother's keeper. We cannot expect someone else to do the job for us.

6

A SHOPPING MALL OF COMPASSION

n 1858, Rowland Macy had a fresh new idea. He realized that people could spend hours—maybe even a full day—shopping for their various necessities. They visited a clothing store for clothing, a grocery store for food, a dry-goods store for fabrics and supplies, a furniture store for furniture, a haberdashery for hats, and so on. He wondered what would happen if someone built one huge store that carried all these items and more. Could this store become a one-stop destination and meet most of the needs that consumers have? With this vision in mind, Macy built the world's first department store in New York City. It had several floors of merchandise— almost anything a person could want and need, all in one place! Of course, it was a rousing success and changed the way people thought about shopping. In our own time, stores like Walmart and Fred Meyer carry on the same tradition.

Might our churches learn something from this model?

Why Does It Exist?

A man named John was trying to repair his car. While he was trying to loosen a bolt on the starter, the wrench slipped, and he badly cut his finger on a sharp piece of metal. He tried to stop the bleeding, but it was just bad enough that he thought he might need stitches. His wife, Melinda, took him to the hospital to have his finger treated. She waited patiently in the car while he went in.

As John entered the emergency room, he was confronted with two doors. The sign above one done read Men, and the other read Women. He walked through the door that read Men.

On the other side of the door was another set of doors. This time the doors read Injury Above the Waist and Injury Below the Waist. He shook his head in puzzlement but continued through the Injury Above the Waist door.

But there he found yet another pair of doors, one reading Serious Injury and the other, Not-So-Serious Injury. He glanced at his finger and proceeded through the door that read Not-So-Serious Injury, only to find himself back in the hospital parking lot.

A rather stunned John walked back to the car where his wife had been waiting. She looked at the shock on his face and the untreated finger and asked, "John, what happened? Did they help you?"

"No," he replied, "but they sure were organized!"

This hospital's mission was to help people in need. It had a beautiful building, all the latest medical technology, a trained staff, and a carefully organized system for dealing with the flow of patients. But they failed to meet their mission because they didn't really meet needs. People like John didn't get the help they needed.

Of course, this is a silly little story, but it's a good reminder that just having a building with a sign on it doesn't mean you are helping anyone. Sadly, many churches are kind of like this hospital. They have beautiful buildings, well designed for aesthetic impact. They have plush seating and the latest multimedia equipment. Their trained and educated staff and organization may function like a "well-oiled machine." But if people are not finding hope and healing, why does the church exist?

Faith and Hope

Whenever a church is willing to confront the needs of its community, it has the opportunity to be the kind of church our world so desperately needs. Rick Warren, writing about the growing movement for churches to become centers that meet people's needs, suggested that "the first reformation...was about creeds; this one's going to be about our deeds. The first one divided the church; this time it will unify the church."[1]

I have a vision for more and more churches becoming "shopping malls of compassion," places where a great variety of human needs can be met—all in one place!—while people also have the opportunity to meet the risen Jesus. As we reach out and take the hands of those in need, Jesus' love becomes real. The power of Christ will not have to squeak through a creed or a theology, but will burst through actions of mercy and compassion and care.

Despite many well-intentioned government programs, poverty has grown in our country. Many of these programs do a lot of good, but they alone cannot solve the problem. Our government has been trying to provide hope without faith, and it will not work. Hebrews 11:1 (KJV) says, "Faith is the substance of things hoped for, the evidence of things not seen." Simply put, faith makes hope possible; faith is the root system of hope. Since 1965, our government has spent more than $9 trillion combating poverty, yet we still lead all industrialized nations in social brokenness. Our government is staffed with many qualified, compassionate, and godly people. But as an institution, it has been trying to provide hope without faith, and hope is not something government can provide. The church is the steward of hope.

I was asked to participate in a roundtable discussion that included the secular media and faith-based leaders. We wanted to find ways the religious community can work better with the media to educate the general public on the plight of the poor. The group of 30 members of the clergy and 15 representatives from the media convened in Washington DC for what would become a lively discussion.

"With all due respect," a journalist for a nationally known newspaper said, "I believe you would be much more effective communicating to the American people if you would communicate less Jesus and more about the needs in the world."

I couldn't let that slide. I stood and made eye contact with the journalist. Many of the clergy turned to see what kind of religious fanatic would take up that kind of challenge.

"The Bible says, 'Faith is the substance of things hoped for,'" I insisted. "That means the root system of hope is faith in Jesus Christ. You cannot have true lasting hope without Jesus. If you take the faith out of 'faith-based,' you no longer have 'the way, the truth, and the life.' Our service to the poor is *for* Jesus and needs to be *through* Jesus if those in need are to experience a holistic transformation."

Our communities need our churches to step up and become faith-based shopping malls of compassion. Lives will not be permanently transformed through government initiatives. Rather, hundreds of churches must accept responsibility to be Christ's merchants of compassion.

Walmart Churches

Regardless of what you may think about Walmart, the world's largest corporation, you'd probably agree that a large component of its success is that it is a "one-stop shop" for just about everything you need—or think you need! Groceries, tires, plants, clothing, DVDs, toys, household supplies, appliances...they're all in one place.

In the same way, the church can respond to people's needs of all kinds—whether spiritual, emotional, relational, or physical. The number of these "Walmart" churches in America is growing, and they are becoming epicenters for spiritual and social renewal in their communities.

One outstanding example of such a vision is People for People, started by a Baptist congregation in north central Philadelphia. Led by Pastor Herb Lusk, this ministry was founded on a vision of bringing transformation to its community. For more than 15 years, People for People has helped low-income individuals leave behind their dependency on welfare through a variety of programs, including help for substance abusers, counseling, education, job training, and teaching computer skills. They have also put a focus on the upcoming generation by developing programs for kids and have worked to help orphans and vulnerable children both in Philadelphia and sub-Saharan Africa.

Their innovative approach includes a member-owned credit union that promotes the financial well-being of low-income families. In an area where poverty and unemployment are high and the majority of households are single-parent families, the traditional financial institutions are not structured to meet the financial needs of the less privileged. Through education about personal finances, services for those who have never had a bank account, nonpredatory short-term loans, SEED accounts for precollege children, and other initiatives, low-income families are given a hand to lift them up to a new level of financial security and responsibility.

People for People also offers an extensive mentoring program for kids. Believing that children are the hope of the future, and realizing the emotional deficit to be found in many single-parent homes, the Children of Promise program matches mentors with children who need another responsible adult in their lives to help them toward greater emotional and relational security.

These are just a couple of examples of the rich variety of ways in which People for People is meeting very practical needs in its community and providing spiritual hope through Jesus Christ. Their impact in their city has been tremendous and transforming!

Standing in the Gap in Pennsylvania

While People for People is busy ministering in an urban setting, the Family Center in Gap, Pennsylvania, is demonstrating how the church can be a shopping mall of compassion in a suburban or rural area. Gap is a small rural community located outside Lancaster, with a rich history that dates back to William Penn's first visit to the area. Founded by Jonas and Anne Beiler, founders of Auntie Anne's Pretzels, the Family Center exists to help families thrive by providing a hub of interactive services that offer a healing presence, foster healthy relationships, and model community cooperation. Their successful programs include a crisis pregnancy center, a learning center, and a day care center.

They also have established some rather unique ministries. The Tree of Life Health Ministry teaches parishioners how they can become healthier by using food-based supplements, learning stress management, and exercising. They provide educational opportunities, a sauna, cleansing therapies, and much more, all with the goal of improving the health of their congregation. Another interesting program is their partnership with the county to provide a high-quality library for their community. This church is marked by a truly holistic vision of Christ impacting every area of life!

Kingdom Diplomacy

Of course, not every church is large enough to maintain a lot of programs by itself. That is where kingdom diplomacy comes into play. We have the opportunity to build collaborations between churches, businesses, and nonprofit organizations. What we can't do alone, we might be able to accomplish together! As the African proverb says, "If you want to go fast, go alone. If you want to go far, go together."

A supernatural synergy occurs when brothers and sisters unite around the mission of sharing the gospel in both word and deed. Kingdom-minded leaders realize that by building bridges across denominational and ethnic lines, their own ministry will be enriched and enlarged. Of course, sometimes this is easier said than done.

While speaking to a group of church leaders about our organization, I got this question from the audience: "Convoy of Hope is working in some of the most dangerous areas in America. Have you ever had an altercation?"

I thought for a moment. "Just one," I admitted. "But fortunately we were able to separate the two pastors."

The group laughed at the joke, but we all knew that trying to unite pastors of diverse ethnicities and denominational affiliations is no laughing matter. Kary Kingsland, Convoy's vice president of disaster response, likes to say, "Unifying faith-based leaders around an outreach or response to disaster victims is the most challenging—yet rewarding—part of our mission." One leader of a nonprofit organization confided in me, "It's much easier to avoid the church politics and get the work done ourselves."

Tragically, many pastors have never even met most of their co-laborers in their own cities and towns, let alone partnered with them for the good of the community. Fearful of the possibility that they might lose a member to another church, some pastors insulate themselves and their congregations. When they do, they also insulate themselves from having the kind of impact their church could have.

We need the kind of kingdom diplomacy that allows us to treasure our own traditions and distinctives and yet empowers us to work together for the common cause of doing Christ's compassionate work in the world. The body of Christ needs every member participating in His servant ministry. We need to learn the character qualities that make cooperation possible, the same qualities that the apostle Paul urged the early Christians to adopt: "Be completely humble and gentle; be patient, bearing with one another in love. Make every effort to keep the unity of the Spirit through the bond of peace. There is one body and one Spirit—just as you were called to one hope when you were called" (Ephesians 4:2-4).

Compassion can break down all kinds of walls. In 2008 I toured the cities along the Gaza border with Joel Rosenberg (a bestselling author who has worked with some of the world's most influential leaders). In this area where Jews and Arabs are constantly at war with each other, residents are awakened almost every morning with sirens warning them of incoming rockets. All around us we saw the craters from the constant bombardment of missiles and mortars. Joel founded Joshua Fund to offer humanitarian relief to Israel and its neighbors.

I was especially impressed with Joshua Fund's support of Barzilai Medical

Center in the southern city of Ashkelon, which serves both Jewish and Arab victims of sickness or of the daily violence. Their medical assistance does not differentiate between the two warring peoples. Joel is a tremendous example of a kingdom diplomat who unites the Christian community to show compassion that transcends politics, race, or culture.

"To keep the unity of the Spirit through the bond of peace"—that is why Convoy of Hope serves local leaders and their ministries, regardless of the differences, risks, and challenges. Over the years, we have been privileged to be a catalyst for unifying pastors and lay leaders through citywide outreaches and disaster relief efforts. It is exciting to see a Baptist pastor, an Episcopal priest, and an Assembly of God preacher all working together to further the message of God's love and compassion. Their example of cooperation sends a message of its own.

WHAT CAN I DO? SOME PRACTICAL WAYS TO MAKE A DIFFERENCE...

- Talk with your pastor about starting a compassion program at your church, such as a food pantry, life-skills counseling, job training, or teaching English as a second language.

- Meet with a few friends and brainstorm ideas for building bridges to churches that are different from yours (that is, churches of different ethnicity, denomination, or socioeconomic makeup).

- Host a conference to train volunteers on ways they can serve the poor.

I'm Ready to Listen

During a 15-hour flight to Africa from Washington DC, I was seated next to a woman who made it clear right away that she had no interest in talking to her fellow passengers. As she squeezed into the seat next to me, she pulled the airline magazine out of the seat pocket and started reading it, oblivious to everyone else around her.

A short time into the flight, I pulled a copy of the brand-new Convoy of Hope brochure out of my bag so I could see how it had come out. As I was giving it a thorough read, I noticed that the woman kept glancing over to see what I was looking at. She initially seemed to want to hide her interest, but eventually her curiosity got the best of her.

"What is it you do?" she enquired.

"I serve with an organization called Convoy of Hope, which provides food, clean water, and hope to people around the world," I answered.

"Is this a religious thing?"

"We're a faith-based organization, but we work with many different denominations and businesses."

"Oh." That seemed like the end of the conversation. About an hour later she looked over at me again. "Why do you do it? Why do you help these children?"

"Well," I said, "I am a follower of Jesus and believe that He commissioned us to help the poor. And I admit, I receive a lot of satisfaction from helping others."

For the next hour she questioned me about Convoy of Hope. When the conversation began to shift into more spiritual matters than she could tolerate, she cut me short. "A lot of people have tried to tell me about Jesus, and I've made clear I am not interested."

I smiled and settled back against the window, closing my eyes to get a little rest. When I awoke I noticed that she had taken the brochure out of my seat pocket and was reading it for herself. "Do you have any more questions?" I asked.

"Yes," she admitted. "I'm ready to listen about Jesus...because of what you do."

When people like this woman discover that the church is relevant to the needs of the world, they are more willing to listen to the good news of the whole gospel. Before we landed, this woman prayed with me to ask Jesus to be her Savior—as did her husband, who was seated on the other side of her and had been listening to the entire conversation.

Our demonstration of God's love in our care to the poor sends a message to a watching world that our gospel is not just a theology or an ideology, not just an abstract idea or something to fight over. Our gospel is a message of transforming love, calling us to be the hands and feet of Jesus as He continues His work of compassion through us. It speaks to nonbelievers in ways that our sermons never will. As Francis of Assisi is reported to have said, "Preach the gospel at all times. When necessary, use words."

7

PRO-LIFE FOR
THE POOR

J esus commanded us to care for "the least of these," but sadly, we must admit that sometimes many of our churches have cared the least. Probably no segment of the population has more closely identified itself with the pro-life message than evangelical Christians. We have stood up for the rights of the unborn with great fervor and passion. We have preached sermons, written books, and sometimes even taken to the streets to defend the rights of unborn children who cannot stand up for themselves.

But we have often used too limited a definition of what it means to be pro-life. We have tended to focus on one issue—abortion—and failed to think carefully enough about what it means to be consistently and thoroughly pro-life. We must not only protect the child in the womb but also save the child living in the slums who is suffering from inadequate food, limited medical care, and subhuman living conditions. If care for the poor was a priority throughout the Bible, should it not be a priority for us today? How can we ignore the truth that our Savior and Redeemer is pro-life for the poor?

How Much Is a Life Worth?

According to the international standard for most private and government-run health insurance plans worldwide, $50,000 is the value of a human life for one year. This figure is used to determine whether to cover a new medical procedure. For the United States military, the value of a human life is $500,000, the "death benefit the government pays families when a soldier is killed in Iraq or Afghanistan."[1]

To God, however, human life is priceless and precious! King David understood his value to God:

> You made all the delicate, inner parts of my body and knit me together in my mother's womb. Thank you for making me so wonderfully complex! Your workmanship is marvelous—how well I know it. You watched me as I was being formed in utter seclusion; as I was woven together in the dark of the womb. You saw me before I was born. Every day of my life was recorded in your book. Every moment was laid out before a single day had passed (Psalms 139:13-16 NLT).

Rick Warren reminds us that God is "Pro-life with a Purpose":

> God never does anything accidentally, and he never makes mistakes. He has a reason for everything he creates. Every plant and every animal was planned by God for a purpose, and every person was designed with a purpose in mind, too. God's motive for creating you is to be the object of his love. The Bible says, "Long before he laid down earth's foundations, he had us in mind, had settled on us as the focus of his love." God was thinking of you even before he made the world. In fact, that's why he created it! God designed this planet's environment so we could live in it. We are the focus of his love and the most valuable of all his creation. The Bible says, "God decided to give us life through the word of truth so we might be the most important of all the things he made." This is how much God loves and values you! God is not haphazard; he planned it all with great precision."[2]

The more that physicists, biologists, and other scientists learn about the universe, the better we understand how it is uniquely suited for human existence, custom-made with the exact specifications that make our life possible. Dr. Michael Denton, senior research fellow in human molecular genetics at the University of Otago in New Zealand, has concluded, "All the evidence available in the biological sciences supports the core proposition...that the cosmos is a specially designed whole, with life and mankind as its fundamental goal and purpose, a whole in which all facets of reality have their meaning and explanation in this central fact." The Bible, of course, said the same thing thousands of years earlier.

The Battle for Life

Jesus said, "The thief's purpose is to steal and kill and destroy. My purpose is to give them a rich and satisfying life" (John 10:10 NLT). The life that Jesus speaks of is eternal, but it begins immediately upon receiving Jesus, who is Himself "the way and the truth and the life" (John 14:6). Like a thief, Satan uses his arsenal of violence, disease, hunger, and other effects of poverty to steal and kill. If he cannot kill, he will devalue a human life so a person merely subsists without being productive to society. The enemy also influences our culture to devalue lives that are not deemed useful to society, labeling them as expendable.

From the beginning of time this has been the satanic strategy: to fight a pro-life God by diminishing the value of His creation. The same enemy was at work in the Nazi concentration camps, which killed six million Jews. The thief was behind the slave trade that snatched millions of men, women, and children from their homes in Africa and transported them in slave ships across the Atlantic to either the Caribbean Islands or North and South America. Hundreds of thousands died en route, and many more were killed by plantation owners. Today, the thief's weapons of mass destruction are not only abortion and euthanasia but also our unwillingness to do something about the death and destruction of the poorest of the poor.

> The world we live in is under siege—three billion are desperately poor, one billion hungry, millions are trafficked into human slavery, ten million children die needlessly each year, wars and conflicts are wreaking havoc, pandemic diseases are spreading, ethnic hatred is flaming and terrorism is growing.[3]

The manifestations of this battle for life might be abortion, euthanasia, sex trafficking, and poverty, but at its root is a spiritual battle for life. The apostle Paul reminds us of the nature of our fight: "For our struggle is not against flesh and blood, but against the rulers, against the authorities, against the powers of this dark world and against spiritual forces of evil in the heavenly realms" (Ephesians 6:12). In the face of such a spiritual battle, God wants to deploy His spiritual warriors to defend the rights and dignities of

His children. "When the enemy shall come in like a flood, the Spirit of the Lord shall lift up a standard against him" (Isaiah 59:19 kjv). We are that "standard" the Spirit of the Lord is lifting up to defend life and help people experience what Jesus described as "a rich and satisfying life."

Good News for the Poor

Jesus told His disciples, "My command is this: Love each other as I have loved you. Greater love has no one than this, that he lay down his life for his friends" (John 15:12-13). Jesus challenged His disciples to love each other as much as He loved them—even to the point of dying for them. God may not necessarily be calling you or me to die for someone, but He is calling us to practice sacrificial love for those who are victims of injustice and are powerless to defend their rights to live with dignity.

Some would contend that defending such rights is the role of government. Thomas Jefferson thought so: "The care of human life and happiness, and not their destruction, is the first and only object of good government." The governments of our world have an important role to play in valuing and protecting every human life, but God calls His people to take the lead in helping others to live "a rich and satisfying life."

When God made a covenant to have an intimate relationship with the Israelites, the people He chose, He gave them laws to live by that were holy and healthy and just. Many of them protected the poor and underprivileged and made provision for their needs. God wanted His people to be different—set apart from the cultures surrounding them, which neglected the impoverished. He also wanted them to be different from cultures that thought the only good use of a foreigner or alien was to enslave them. Leviticus 25:35-36 is a good summary of God's pro-life perspective:

> If one of your countrymen becomes poor and is unable to support himself among you, help him as you would an alien or a temporary resident, so he can continue to live among you. Do not take interest of any kind from him, but fear your God, so that your countrymen may continue to live among you.

Then God poignantly states His goal: "There should be no poor among you" (Deuteronomy 15:4), but "there will always be poor people in the land. Therefore I command you to be openhanded toward your brothers and toward the poor and needy in your land" (Deuteronomy 15:11).

When Jesus announces His mission, He quotes from Isaiah 61 to announce what He came to do:

> The Spirit of the Lord is on me,
>   because he has anointed me
>   to preach good news to the poor.
> He has sent me to proclaim freedom for the prisoners
>   and recovery of sight for the blind,
> to release the oppressed,
>   to proclaim the year of the Lord's favor (Luke 4:18-19).

Ultimately, Jesus' mission of good news was to save mankind from sin so we could live with Him eternally. But the good news was not only about the life to come but also about the quality of our earthly life as well. The good news to people in bondage was freedom, and to the sick, it was healing. He announced His mission to preach the good news to the poor and then challenged his disciples to slip into His sandals and do the same.

WHAT CAN I DO? SOME PRACTICAL WAYS TO MAKE A DIFFERENCE...

- Treat every person you meet today as a unique and precious gift from the Lord.
- Host or participate in a pro-life rally.
- Coordinate an annual "Bless a Child Day" at your church that educates people on ways they can become more pro-life for the poor.

In the next several chapters, you will read about the daunting battles we face in combating poverty, homelessness, hunger, and other great evils. You'll read about the heartrending realities faced by children and their families who live in extreme poverty, whether in the streets of Nairobi, Kenya, or the slums of Calcutta, India. We'll also see the sad truth about how many American families are also struggling with poverty and homelessness right in our own cities and towns. And you'll be brought face-to-face with the sad realities facing orphans here and abroad.

As you read about some harsh truths, I hope that the bad news will not overshadow the good news that we can do something about all this suffering. We'll look at the promises of Scripture and the inspirational stories of people who are finding hope in the midst of great misery. More than anything else, I hope you will be challenged to become one of God's warriors who are joining in the fight against these great evils.

Rick Warren put it best: "You don't judge the strength of an army by how many soldiers sit and eat in the mess hall, but by how they perform on the front line. Likewise a church's strength is not seen in how many show up for services (the crowd) but in how many serve in the core."[4] The compassion revolution is good news for the poor. At the forefront of the revolution stands Jesus, beckoning you and me to become actively pro-life.

"IS THIS HEAVEN?"
Caring for Orphans

The Kenya Kids Home in Nairobi is a refuge for kids who have lost their parents to disaster or disease, or who have simply been abandoned when their families could no longer care for them. The founder, Peter Njiri, is a leader I greatly admire for his heart and compassion. Every day he comes face-to-face with the heartbreaking realities of how lives are destroyed by need and deprivation. His work could become disheartening, but he is often reminded of how much good can be done by meeting the simplest but deepest needs.

One evening, his director for the Kenya Kids Home opened the front door of the orphanage and discovered a filthy, battered, and dangerously malnourished little boy who had been abandoned on his steps. Perhaps desperate parents had left him there because they had run out of options and could no longer feed and look after him. Or maybe the young boy had been fending for himself for a long time and had finally gone to the only place where he thought he might get help. Either way, he was very weak and frail. Realizing that the young lad could barely stand up, the director scooped him up in his arms and carried him inside.

Having lived so long on the streets, the boy was afraid to go into the building. But the director and other workers treated him with great gentleness as they scrubbed off the layers of dirt and gave him a hot meal, which he scarfed down with abandon. He obviously hadn't eaten much in a very long time.

Then it was time for bed, so the director led him down the hall to the dorm room, which had several rows of bunk beds. The director laid him down on a vacant bed and told him soothingly, "We do not know who left you on our doorstep, but you are safe here, and we will take care of you."

Pulling back the covers, the director slipped the boy's fragile bony legs underneath. "This is your bed," he said, and kissed the boy on the forehead. "You are safe here. Go to sleep."

During bed checks later that night, the director was startled to see the boy's bed empty. He and his staff searched for the missing child. When they found him, he was not outside and had not run away. In the darkness, they had overlooked him lying on the floor beside the bed. The director picked him up and tucked him back in the bed.

"Why were you sleeping on the floor?" he asked.

"I have never slept in a bed," the boy answered quietly. Then, with tears filling his scared but hopeful eyes, he asked, "Is this heaven?"

God's Short List

In the time it takes you to read this sentence, four children will lose a parent due to poverty, disease, violence, or a natural disaster. According to the United Nations, the number of children (between ages three and eighteen) living on the streets is about 150 million—and rising daily. This alarming statistic should give us pause, especially when we consider the priority given to caring for orphans in Scripture. In the letter of James it is actually part of the definition of a faith approved by God: "Religion that God our Father accepts as pure and faultless is this: to look after orphans and widows in their distress and to keep oneself from being polluted by the world" (James 1:27). This passage of Scripture is like a huge billboard in our path to remind us that caring for orphans is on God's short list of priorities.

If you are contemplating your priorities as a church or a denomination, keep this verse in mind. When envisioning a bigger and more beautiful edifice, employing more staff, or expanding your programs, consider this verse and ask yourself, what about the orphans? When you are planning budgets or considering some new technique for church growth, ask yourself, What about the orphans? How can we read James 1:27 and not make caring for orphans a centerpiece of our mission? Where else in the Bible is it made so clear what kind of faith in action is pleasing to God?

Who Will Get to Them First?

The need is urgent. Every day, every minute, precious young lives are slipping away. The race is not only for the survival of these orphans but also for their rescue before they are recruited by warlords and terrorists. Radical groups like Al Qaeda find an inexhaustible supply of children and youth among the orphans to help them carry on their campaigns of terror. Surely the images of small boys carrying automatic weapons and artillery are some of the most disturbing of our time. These boys are recruited into militias, where they get their primary needs met, receive recognition, and find a sense of purpose in exchange for becoming young killing machines.

The innocence of youth is also stolen from young girls, who are pressed into service as prostitutes to serve the sexual desires of the soldiers. "An estimated 250,000 children are involved in conflicts around the world. They are used as combatants, messengers, spies, porters, cooks, and girls in particular are forced to perform sexual services, depriving them of their rights and their childhood."[1]

Young girls are forced into prostitution.

Most of the children living in underdeveloped countries face three potential futures: death from hunger and disease, conscription by evil dictators and warlords, or rescue—being fed, clothed, and educated so they can be part of bringing about change among their own people. Reaching the children means hope for a better life for future generations. Failing to care for the children ensures the continuation of the devastating cycle of despair.

Our obedience to God's command to care for the orphans can determine which path many children will follow. Job, the biblical character who learned to trust in God through suffering, understood the priority of orphans and made caring for them a centerpiece of his life: "Whoever heard me spoke well of me, and those who saw me commended me, because I rescued the poor who cried for help, and the fatherless who had none to assist him…I was a father to the needy; I took up the case of the stranger. I broke the fangs of the wicked and snatched the victims from their teeth" (Job 29:11-12,16-17). Are you prepared, like Job, to help snatch the world's orphans from the jaws of hunger, poverty, manipulation, and degradation?

A "HopeWalk" Through the Slums

The Kenya Kids Home provides one of the finest models I have seen for helping orphans. They don't just settle for meeting the immediate needs of these young people, but help them build a future for themselves. They take care of about 80 children at a time, most of them for at least two years. During their time in the Kenya Kids Home, the children receive counseling and attend informal schooling, which prepares them for later entry into public schools. They also learn about God's love, sing in a choir, memorize Scripture, and develop basic life skills, such as proper hygiene and good manners.

The goal is to prepare them for a productive life by building a foundation of knowledge and emotional security. These children feel safe because they experience genuine love and caring from the staff of the orphanage. The Kenya Kids Home reflects the atmosphere and culture of Africa and does not squeeze kids into a Western mold.

After one year, the children are transferred, ten or twelve at a time, to a group home that is connected to a local church. From there they are placed in families and are ready to take their place as secure and productive members of their society.

On behalf of Convoy of Hope, I like to take business leaders and pastors to Africa and Latin America, where they can see what poverty is really like. We call these visits HopeWalks. I have seen again and again how these experiences change people, how they motivate folks to get involved when they see that poverty has a name, a face, and eyes looking back at them. Following his African adventure, Michael Kern, president and COO of Stout Risius Ross, reflected on his experience:

> As our team journeyed through Kenya's Mathare Valley—one of the world's poorest communities—I saw, heard, smelled, felt, and experienced things that destroyed the barriers separating my isolated world from the impoverished one I was walking through. It's one thing to hear about hungry children; it's another to look them in the eyes. Though I knew beforehand that I would encounter all these things, I never expected my life, goals, ambitions, dreams, and heart to be so utterly transformed by what I experienced.[2]

Kenya's Mathare Valley children living in slums.

After his HopeWalk, Michael had to do something. So he and his wife, Amanda, sponsored the building of a group home. They partnered with the Kenya Assemblies of God and a local church to provide a trained couple to serve as the group home parents and to cover the ongoing operating costs. Michael and Amanda hope the children in their group home will grow up in a nurturing environment to become doctors, teachers, ministers, and missionaries to their own people.

Don't Remove the Tags!

One of the great needs of orphans is for clothing to protect them from the effects of hot and cold weather. When Jesus talks about ways we can reach out to the least of these, He specifically mentions clothing: "I needed clothes and you clothed me" (Matthew 25:36). But clothes do more than merely protect children from the effects of the weather and the spread of disease—they also build dignity and self-confidence. I have seen this dynamic in action for myself.

"Please don't remove the tags!"

I remember kneeling down to help a needy child in Kenya put on a brand-new pair of shoes. Her face beamed as I slipped on first one and then the other shoe. But when I reached down to tear off the tags that were attached, she began to cry. Confused, I asked her teacher why she was so upset with me.

"Well," said the teacher in a tone that showed she was also a bit unhappy with me, "she has never had anything new before, and the tags are the proof. So we keep the tags!"

I immediately apologized and tied those tags right back on. The girl's face lit up again.

When I returned a couple months later, as you'd expect, the shiny black shoes were flocked with dust from the Mathare Valley. Yet to my delight and amazement, the tags were still hanging from the shoes!

Shoes of Hope

Our vision to provide shoes for poor children was born when my brother Hal visited the Mathare Children's Development Center (MCDC) in Nairobi, Kenya. He was deeply moved to see how many children had no shoes to protect their feet from injury, diseases, or the ravages of the weather, and he was determined to do something about it. On his return he announced his intention to the Convoy of Hope leadership team: "We are going to provide a new pair of shoes to every one of these children."

With the help of his daughter Lindsay, he started "Shoes of Hope," which continues to this day to raise money to buy shoes for poor children around the world. The initial funds were raised and wired to the leaders of the MCDC so that they could purchase shoes and socks for 400 children. I was going to be in Nairobi later that month, so the African leaders asked if I would personally present the shoes to the children. I said that it would be a pleasure. And it was.

When I walked into the meeting hall at the MCDC, I saw four-foot high stacks of white and yellow boxes containing socks and shoes. As the children filed into the room, they were smiling, giggling with excitement, and pointing at the wall of boxes. I opened one of the boxes and held a shoe up for them all to see. "This is a special day for those who purchased these shoes for you. We believe that when you walk in them you will walk for Jesus and know that there are people thousands of miles away who love you very much."

The children lined up, from the youngest to the oldest, and received their shoes. One little boy who came forward was dressed in ragged clothes that spoke of the depth of his need. As he sat down in the chair opposite me, I knelt down in front of him and opened a box. That was when I noticed the shoes that he had on—a pair of discolored yellow flip-flops that were probably twice the size of his feet. I took them off and placed them on the ground before slipping on the new socks and shoes. His eyes sparkled with glee.

When I stood to receive the next child in line, I felt a gentle tug at my shirt.

The little boy was looking up at me and stretching his worn flip-flops toward my hands. "Sir," he said, "please take these shoes to children who have none."

I fought back tears as I looked at this little boy who, at the moment of receiving shoes, was thinking about other children who had none. I thought of the walk-in closets in my own home and those of my friends, filled with shoes and clothes that reflect our every whim of fashion. We spend thousands of dollars to mirror the latest styles while many in the world have but one change of clothes.

Every year six million of these infants and toddlers die as a result of hunger.

WHAT CAN I DO? SOME PRACTICAL WAYS TO MAKE A DIFFERENCE...

- Go on a mission trip that will help orphans.

- Provide financial support for charities that help orphans (see appendix 3 for recommended compassion organizations).

- Become a monthly sponsor for a child through a compassion organization.

- Educate people in your church, job, or school on the plight of orphans and practical ways they can make a difference.

The Speech That Never Was

The need will not wait, and the time to act is now. Are you willing to help those who are working to meet the needs of orphans?

When I was in high school, my teacher assigned each student in my class a topic to research in preparation for a class presentation. She gave me the topic of procrastination and assigned a date for my presentation.

The day arrived, and she called on me. "Donaldson, you're next with the topic of procrastination." I slowly and reluctantly stood to my feet. Instead of making my way to the front of the class, I halted in front of the teacher. "Would it be possible for me to present my speech on another day? I have been swamped with other schoolwork and chores at home, so I haven't had time to prepare."

Someone from the back of the class spoke up: "Hey c'mon, we had to give ours!"

A rumble of chuckles spread across the room, and my teacher looked annoyed. "If I give you extra time, I'll have to give extra time to all the students. That isn't possible. You'll just have to give it your best shot."

"Can I please do it next week?" I begged.

"No. You need to do it now."

The whole class started laughing, not very sympathetic to the situation. I started to plead, "Please? What about tomorrow?"

She was out of patience. "If you don't do it today, you'll receive an incomplete for this project."

"Okay then," now trying to make a deal, "what about pushing my presentation to the end of the class so that I have more time to think through my speech?"

Now exasperated, she laid her head on the desk and mumbled something about wishing she had chosen a different line of work. After a long sigh, she picked up her pen and said, "I am going to just give you an incomplete."

"Wait, wait…I'll do it." I walked to the podium, paused for a moment to gather myself, and smiled at the teacher and the class. "You have just seen my presentation on procrastination."

The class roared its approval, and she just shook her head and smiled. "I guess I'll have to forgive you for raising my blood pressure because that was the most persuasive presentation of a topic I have ever seen."

Maybe it is not a tragedy to procrastinate about a school assignment or some yard work that needs to be done. But it is tragic to think of the precious young lives being warped or lost every day. We must not procrastinate. We can't just wait on the sidelines and hope things will get better. Of course, we cannot save all of the orphans right now, but we can rescue many. When Michael Kern saw the need for himself, he got involved, and now he encourages others to do the same. The urgency of the need is matched only by the deep satisfaction of knowing you are doing something to help. We have the opportunity to give boys and girls a chance to live, laugh, and succeed. We have the expertise, the resources, and the compassion to save a generation from extinction. There is no time for procrastination. Every moment counts. Let's give orphans a little glimpse of heaven.

"PLEASE TAKE MY BABY!"
Feeding the Hungry

A s we made our way through Calcutta's Victoria Square, our driver spotted a street vendor offering cold drinks. The heat had been oppressive all morning, and we were all thirsty. Finding a place to pull off, he got out of the car and made his way to the vendor to get us each a Coke. I was feeling too hot to want to move, so I remained in the car with my window rolled down.

I sat there taking in the rush and bustle of crowds of people scrambling through the market area. Some were shopping, some were hawking their goods, some were begging for food or money. My arm was hanging out the window, my eyes drifting through the crowd. Suddenly I felt a sharp tug at my sleeve.

Turning my head, I met the eyes of a young Indian woman who was pleading with me in a language I could not understand and pointing at the baby she was holding. I fumbled in my pocket for a few coins and handed them to her, thinking she needed money to buy food for her child. But she waved off the money and spoke louder and more insistently, continuing to point. What was the problem? Did she not think I was offering enough?

Frustrated at her ingratitude, I began to roll up my window.

By that time the driver had returned and had watched the whole episode unfold. After he got into the car, he turned toward me. "She does not want your money. She wants you to take her child."

My heart fell to the floor. "Do you mean she wants me to take her child home with me to America?"

"Yes. She believes her baby will die if you do not take him."

I took one more glance at her desperate eyes and then fished out my sunglasses. I was not shielding my eyes from the sun, but hiding my tears.

"Daddy, I'm Hungry"

Can we even begin to imagine feeling so desperate that we would beg someone to take our child in order that he or she might survive? When we consider the lengths our love would drive us on behalf of our own children, can we begin to understand feeling so helpless and hopeless that we would offer them to a stranger? Ron Sider asks similar questions:

> Can we comprehend what it means for poverty-stricken parents to watch with helpless grief as their baby daughter dies of a common childhood disease because they lack access to elementary health services? Can we grasp the awful truth that thirty thousand children die every day of hunger and preventative diseases?[1]

These troubling questions bring home the reality of poverty and its effects. Or try this little mental experiment suggested by Rich Stearns:

> Imagine what it would be like to awaken each morning wondering if you were going to eat. You have no money, there is no food available—you can't just run down to the grocery store. You would awake to the knowledge that every hour of your day must be obsessively devoted to the search for sustenance.[2]

Perhaps we all need to do what John Wesley asked of his followers: "Put yourself in the place of the poor man and deal with him as you would have God deal with you." If we were to do this we couldn't possibly allow ourselves to remain inactive about this devastating problem, which affects countless millions throughout the world; people whose lives are consumed with the desperate search for food to save themselves and their children.

I got an inkling of what this might be like one day on a freeway with my youngest daughter, Brooke. She was only three years old, and we were stopped in bumper-to-bumper traffic.

Brooke started to cry, saying, "Daddy, I'm hungry."

"I'm sorry," I tried to explain, "but we can't get any food right now." Our car was just one in a line of motionless vehicles, and the next exit was three or four miles away.

Her cries grew louder. "Daddy, I'm hungry," she wailed.

I was helpless as my hands grew tight on the steering wheel. "I'm sorry, baby, but Daddy can't do anything about it right now."

Then a realization awakened inside me. I was trying to explain to my daughter why she might have to go hungry for another hour. Yet I knew that if she could be patient, we would find food just down the road. But what if there wasn't food at the next exit—or at any exit we would find? What if I wasn't sure she would ever be able to eat again? I suddenly saw in my mind a mom or dad in Africa, India, or South America listening as their children cry for days on end because their stomachs are churning with hunger pains and the agony of starvation. I saw parents watching helplessly as their children died a slow and agonizing death because they had no food to give them.

This imaginative scenario is not an unusual occurrence in real life. All around the globe, mothers and fathers tuck their children into bed at night, wondering if they will be able to find food for them the next day.

More than 840 million people in the world are malnourished—799 million of them live in the developing world. Of these, more than 153 million are children under the age of five. And every year, six million of these infants and toddlers die as a result of hunger. Others manage to find just enough food to keep them alive but not enough to sustain healthy bodies, so they develop crippling diseases and ailments and are destined to live out their days in pain and need. Undernourishment negatively affects people's health, sense of hope, security, and overall ability to think and be productive. A lack of food can stunt growth, sap energy, and contribute to mental retardation.

The High Cost of Hunger

Our humanitarian impulses do not provide our only motivation to give more attention to the problem of world hunger. We also need to consider the ripple effects of poverty on global stability. If some cannot be moved by the searing human tragedy of poverty, perhaps they can be swayed by considering the way poverty destabilizes the peace and security of the whole world.

Josette Sheeran, director of the United Nations World Food Program, reminds us that "a hungry world is a dangerous world. Without food, people have only three options: they riot, they emigrate, or they die." In 2008 at least 30 countries experienced food riots as hungry people took to the streets. In Haiti these riots turned particularly deadly. Such riots bring further political and economic destabilization, which eventually affect us all.

We can easily understand why terrorists have little problem recruiting the hungry and impoverished to their violent causes. People who believe they may die of hunger are not as afraid of dying in a terrorist act as others are. Desperate people rally to radical political causes more quickly than others. They are much more likely even to go so far as to offer their lives in a sacrificial terrorist act if they believe that it will help the ones they love to have something to eat in the future. Therefore, it is in the best interest of every nation in the human family to cooperate to bring the hunger crisis to an end.

Working to end poverty is not only a matter of human kindness (though it is surely that) but also a matter of practical necessity. Eradicating poverty must become a priority if we are to live in a world that is not only just and equitable but also safe. In his book *The End of Poverty*, Jeffrey Sachs calls us to reevaluate our strategy for making ourselves more secure:

> Since September 11, 2001, the United States has launched a war on terror, but it has neglected the deeper causes of global instability. The $450 billion that the United States will spend this year on the military will never buy peace if it continues to spend around one thirtieth of that, just $15 billion, to address the plight of the world's poorest of the poor, whose societies are destabilized by extreme poverty and thereby become havens of unrest, violence, and even global terrorism.[3]

The solution, according to Sachs, is to help the poorest of the poor to climb up off the lowest rung of the ladder of economic development, not merely by meeting their immediate needs for food, safe water, and health, but by helping build the infrastructure that can assist them to permanently escaping the poverty trap. A 2001 study found that 93 percent of the world's extremely poor lived in three regions: East Asia, South Asia, and sub-Saharan Africa. In Africa, almost half the population is currently deemed to live in extreme poverty. *Half the population!* Droughts and government corruption have exacerbated the awful situation, and there are no simple, quick and easy solutions. But economists like Sachs are suggesting ways that the nations of the world can cooperate together in wise spending to bring lasting change. There may be a significant immediate cost, but that cost is small considering the cost of poor nations continuing to be recruiting grounds for warlords and terrorists.

There Is a Solution

When Jesus was on a preaching mission and being followed by multitudes who wanted to hear the good news of the gospel, He felt moved by their needs. He said to His disciples, "I have compassion for these people; they have already been with me three days and have nothing to eat. I do not want to send them away hungry, or they may collapse on the way" (Matthew 15:32). Surely Jesus feels the same way today: "I do not want to send them away hungry." How can we be exposed to suffering in the world and not be moved as Jesus was?

The good news is that the problem of world hunger is a *solvable* problem.

Rich Stearns sums up the situation well: "The world can and does produce enough food to feed all of its 6.7 billion inhabitants. The problem is that both the food and the capacity to produce it are unequally distributed."[4] While others barely subsist (or fail in the struggle to subsist), Americans have an abundance of food. In the U.S., nearly 100 billion pounds of food—including fresh fruits and vegetables, milk, meat, and grain products—are wasted every year. *One hundred billion pounds!* One 2004 study estimated that the average American household wastes 14 percent of its food purchases. With all the pressing need for food, such a large amount of food being lost to waste and spoilage is a tragedy as well as a commentary on our extravagant lifestyles.

And lest you think that hunger is only a problem overseas, take note of the fact that according to Bread for the World Institute, 3.5 percent of U.S. households experience hunger. Some of these households frequently skip meals or eat too little because of inadequate money to buy food. In all, 9.6 million people live in these homes, including 3 million children. Couple that with the U.S. Census Bureau findings that 35.9 million people in our country live below the poverty line (including 12.9 million children), and you can see that the hunger problem needs to be addressed here at home as well as abroad.

The United Nations Development Program estimates that the basic health and nutrition needs of the world's poorest poor could be met for an additional $13 billion dollars a year. Animal lovers in the U.S. and Europe spend more than that on pet food each year.[5] Each of us needs to ask, *Would I be willing to change some of my priorities so that I have more resources to feed the hungry and save the lives of innocent children and their families?*

God's Plan for Ending Hunger

God's plan for ending world hunger is found in His Word, and it begins with you and me making different choices about how we live. Everyone is blessed with God-given resources. The firstfruits or first 10 percent of our harvest or income should go to our local church (Malachi 3:10). But that should not be the sum total of our giving. It is just the start. Generosity should be a way of life. Hebrew farmers were to make some of their produce available to the poor: "When you reap the harvest of your land, do not reap to the very edges of your field or gather the gleanings of your harvest. Leave them for the poor and the alien. I am the LORD your God" (Leviticus 23:22). This practice is illustrated in the story of Ruth (Ruth 2). Her relative Boaz obeys God's command and leaves the corners of his field unharvested and the upper branches of their fruit trees unpicked so that the poor will have an opportunity to work and survive.

If we apply this principle to our own times, it would remind us that a portion of what we have belongs to the poor. Our abundance is not meant to be hoarded for ourselves, but to be shared with others, especially those in need.

Deuteronomy 24 provides a good summary of this principle:

> Do not deprive the alien or the fatherless of justice, or take the cloak of the widow as a pledge. Remember that you were slaves in Egypt and the LORD your God redeemed you from there. That is why I command you to do this.
>
> When you are harvesting in your field and you overlook a sheaf, do not go back to get it. Leave it for the alien, the fatherless and the widow, so that the LORD your God may bless you in all the work of your hands. When you beat the olives from your trees, do not go over the branches a second time. Leave what remains for the alien, the fatherless and the widow. When you harvest the

grapes in your vineyard, do not go over the vines again. Leave what remains for the alien, the fatherless and the widow. Remember that you were slaves in Egypt. That is why I command you to do this (Deuteronomy 24:17-22).

Note the progression in Deuteronomy 24:

1. The need. "Do not deprive the alien or the fatherless of justice" (verse 17). It is an injustice when anyone, especially a child or an elderly person, is trapped by poverty and malnourishment through no fault of their own. We are responsible to defend the God-given rights of children to be protected and sustained through nutritious food and clean, safe water. This is part of what it means to be pro-life for the poor.

2. The motive. "Remember that you were slaves in Egypt and the LORD your God redeemed you from there" (verse 18). What does this have to do with helping the poor? In effect, God is saying to His people, "I rescued you, I dropped down food from heaven, I provided water from a rock, and I even kept your sandals from wearing out. The best way to show your gratitude and praise is to help others who lack these things." Gratefulness is the key motivation for compassion. We give because we have received such blessings in our lives. God has rescued us from the slavery of sin to serve others, and we are able to provide our own children with food, water, clothing, and shelter. The best way to thank God for these blessings is to bless others out of our abundance. Giving to others is an offering of praise to the Lord for His salvation and provision.

3. The commandment. "This is why I command you to do this" (verse 18). God wants us to help the poor out of a heart of praise and thanksgiving. But notice that it is not a suggestion; it is a command.

4. The reward. "So that the LORD your God may bless you in all the work of your hands" (verse 19). Underscore the word *all.* God blesses every area of our lives—not just our finances—when we help the poor. I can't fully explain this, but something supernatural happens when we give to those who cannot possibly pay us back. Remember God's words through the prophet Isaiah:

> If you spend yourselves in behalf of the hungry and satisfy the needs of the oppressed, then your light will rise in the darkness, and your night will become like the noonday. The LORD will guide you always; he will satisfy your needs in a sun-scorched land and

will strengthen your frame. You will be like a well-watered garden, like a spring whose waters never fail (Isaiah 58:10-11).

When we give to the poor, God opens the windows of heaven and blesses *all* the work of our hands. According to the Bible, helping the poor can positively impact every area of our lives. "A generous man will himself be blessed, for he shares his food with the poor" (Proverbs 22:9).

The biblical pattern clearly goes beyond simply meeting a needy person's immediate necessities. It charts a course that leads toward sustainability, toward the goal of empowering people to eventually meet their own needs. God provided manna for the Israelites during their desert wanderings, but its purpose was to sustain them as they marched toward a goal—the promised land (Exodus 16:31-35). Once they got there, the heavenly manna stopped coming, and the people raised their own crops.

We see this echoed in the story of Ruth. Ruth worked in Boaz's field and then was adopted into his household. It is interesting that one of the things that attracted Boaz was her work ethic—"She worked all day long." As we will discuss later, relief must be part of a continuum of care that leads a person and family to sustainability. Convoy of Hope feeds the hungry to meet their immediate need for food, but we also make sure that they hear the gospel message and receive training in nutrition and other life skills.

A Model of Hope: El Salvador

Kenton Moody was working on a Convoy of Hope program at a school in El Salvador when his eyes were drawn to Maria, a beautiful, dark-haired, six-year-old wisp of a girl. She was abnormally thin and looked sad and defeated. She lacked the usual energy of a girl her age. This is common in the developing world, where 26 percent of children under five are moderately to severely underweight, 10 percent are severely underweight, 11 percent are moderately to severely "wasted" (seriously below weight for one's height), and 32 percent are moderately to severely below normal height for their age.

Maria was squatting weakly against a wall in the schoolroom, so Kenton went over to her. "Hey, honey, what's wrong?"

"I'm hungry," she replied weakly.

"Didn't you eat anything at home?"

"No."

"Why not?"

She looked up at Kenton. "There's nobody there to give me anything."

Maria's parents were out working, trying to eke out a living to meet the bare necessities of life...and barely managing. Both of them worked as many hours as possible just to maintain a subsistence level for the family. Consequently, this little child, smaller than her years would warrant, got up alone every morning, dressed herself, and came to her school session without even a morsel of food in her stomach. *How can she possibly be expected to learn if she has to do it on an empty stomach?* Kenton said to himself. He saw to it that she had a good meal that very afternoon. But Kenton knew that this was only a temporary bit of help and that more needed to be done.

Hundreds of children in El Salvador receive a hot and nutritious meal.

Within a couple of years, partly because of Kenton's efforts, Convoy of Hope had partnered with the Liceo Cristiano school system to provide for the needs of school-age children. We saw that education was critical to the future of these children and the development of their nation but that hunger pangs were getting in the way of learning. The program we started provides a nutritious hot meal (for many children their only substantial meal for the day), daily vitamins, antiparasitic medicine, basic health and nutritional training, water purification, and school supplies. Our goal is to get the children off to a strong start educationally so they might make a better future for themselves.

WHAT CAN I DO? SOME PRACTICAL WAYS TO MAKE A DIFFERENCE...

- Become an ambassador for "One Day to Feed the World" (www. convoyofhope.org) at your church, job, or school.

- Encourage your company to donate food and/or funds to support relief organizations.

- Make a point to not waste food.

- Participate in a U.S. outreach or a mission trip that feeds the hungry.

- Consider a one-day fast to identify with the hungry and build spiritual awareness.

A Model of Hope: Mathare Valley Slums

The slums of the Mathare Valley comprise one of the neediest places on earth, where more than 300,000 people are engaged in a daily struggle for survival. My brother Hal describes what he saw on his first visit there:

> Children scavenge for food through piles of slimy trash made warm by the ruthless sun. In rickety shacks, AIDS-stricken mothers cling to their last days of life. On narrow pathways, toddlers lap water from gutters filled with raw sewage. Young children sniff glue to take away their hunger pangs. Narrow streams trickle with raw sewage. Scrawny, listless children scavenge through piles of garbage. Dogs and oversized rats wander in search of food. An entourage of boys and girls forms behind us, each one hoping for a donation of coins or morsels of food.

In the midst of such squalor, disease, and hunger God has placed a haven of hope called Mathare Children Development Center. Hal describes the work they do:

> Peter Nuthu and his wife, Jane, began their outreach to children in the slums by feeding 12 children who helped him complete some work on the church and school property. For months he prayed that God would provide the resources to feed hundreds more street children each day. He recognized the desperate need and the opportunity; he simply didn't know where to find funding. When an article and photographs were published in *Today's Pentecostal Evangel*, readers were given the opportunity to contribute to the expansion of the feeding ministry. Today, Mathare Children Development Center, in partnership with the Kenya Assemblies of God and Convoy of Hope, feeds and clothes more than 400 children, offers medical screenings, and provides boys and girls with an education.[6]

Mathare Children Development Center feeding program—
the only meal they receive each day.

One Day That Changes the World

It is encouraging to see how relief organizations around the world are finding ways to help the starving poor. But you may be wondering, *What can*

I do? What can my church do? The experience of Alamo Christian Assembly in the San Francisco Bay area is a good example of how very much even a small church can help.

One day, Ken Jones, former pastor of Alamo Christian Church, received a mailing from Convoy of Hope that spoke of the immense needs worldwide. His heart was moved to action, and he wanted to do something more than just receive an extra offering at the end of the church service. He wanted to do something that would have a lasting effect.

For two months he preached every Sunday morning on God's compassion for the poor and our responsibility to help them. He emphasized the idea of "leaving a corner," teaching his people about what we owe the impoverished. All this preaching and teaching led up to a challenge—that members of the congregation would give up one day's wages in order to help the poor and the suffering.

Virtually everyone in the church of 200 members caught the vision, from teenagers with part-time jobs to senior citizens living on pensions. When the day came for the offering, those in the pews donated a whopping $22,700.

This initiative, which came to be called "One Day to Feed the World," has since spread to hundreds of churches and businesses. "The idea," says Jones, "is not to feed the world in a day—there is no way we'll ever be able to do that. But we can bring in one day's pay." It is a way to begin to take action against an escalating problem.

With half the world's population living on less than two dollars a day, the need of the hungry grew even more acute as a global recession tightened pocketbooks and dried up giving. In addition, the price of food skyrocketed as food supplies diminished.

In a time when many of us are personally feeling an economic pinch, we dare not forget those whose situation is so much more dire than our own. Clearly, programs like that suggested by Pastor Jones involve sacrificial giving. Since these funds are not in lieu of tithing or regular missions offerings, they challenge people to dig deeper to help. But participating churches have discovered that "One Day to Feed the World" cultivates a spirit of generosity. Amazingly, the year that Alamo Christian Church launched the concept, its general fund grew by 21 percent, and its missions fund grew by 42 percent! When a people begin to give, they soon experience new joy and a sense of purpose. Giving begets giving!

There Is Always Hope

A number of years ago, a Russian submarine sank to the bottom of the ocean and was left without power. Divers were sent to find a way to rescue the crew. When the divers returned to the surface, they reported hearing Morse code. The crew had been tapping on the metal, "Is there any hope?"[7]

Well, I can't speak for those sailors trapped at the bottom of the sea, but I can speak for the hungry masses through the world and those who want to help them. Yes, there is hope! That conviction gives our ministry its name, Convoy of Hope. We know that the God of the universe wills an end to hunger, injustice, and oppression. He has blessed us with the resources and expertise to defeat the predator of hunger, which attacks and kills vulnerable children and the elderly. And He calls you and me to believe in that hope and act upon it.

If the Gospel writer were to quote Jesus in modern times, I believe His admonition in Matthew 25:35-40 might read something like this:

"I showed you the hungry and how you could feed them."

Then the churchgoer will answer Jesus and say, "Lord, when did we see the hungry?"

"I showed you the plight of the starving children through books, the media, and missionary and relief organizations that shared at your church. Listen, I am telling you the truth: You are the one I am counting on to help them. Do it for Me."

10

WATER IS LIFE!

Water is central to human survival. We can live for weeks without food if we absolutely have to. But without water we can only survive for a matter of days. Water is life!

More than a billion people are without safe drinking water worldwide, and a child dies every 15 seconds from water-related diseases. At any one time, half of the world's hospital beds are occupied by patients suffering from waterborne diseases. This is an international crisis much bigger than any tsunami or hurricane could ever be.

In the Western world, we don't give much thought to water. After all, most of us simply turn on the faucet, and out it comes—as much as we need. The typical American family uses about 69 gallons a day. If you have teenagers who like to take long showers, your number is probably higher! And in the average home, nearly 10 gallons are simply wasted each day by leaky pipes and fittings.

Use	Gallons per Capita	Percentage of Total Daily Use
Showers	11.6	16.8%
Clothes Washers	15.0	21.7%
Dishwashers	1.0	1.4%
Toilets	18.5	26.7%
Baths	1.2	1.7%
Leaks	9.5	13.7%
Faucets	10.9	15.7%
Other Domestic Uses	1.6	2.2%[1]

In America we simply turn on the faucet, and water comes out to meet our needs. What if you had to carry nearly 70 gallons of water every day from a water source to your home? Let's do the math: One gallon of water weighs approx 8.32 pounds, so 69.3 gallons equals more than 576 pounds. Think about the impossibility of carrying 576 pounds of water from a lake or stream to your home each and every day! In most third world countries, women and children usually retrieve the water. If the average person could carry 20 pounds of water, she would have to make 29 trips. Of course, the poor are using only a fraction of the amount of water that Americans use, but much of their lives is consumed with trying to gather enough water to survive.

Dying for Water

During droughts, I have experienced the horror of seeing people who have died from the rigors of searching for water. One missionary said, "Over a period of time, when they get less and less rain, people's capacity to rebound is lowered, and they finally reach bottom. They die or just give up." I will never forget the sight of an elderly woman lying dead alongside a road with a container in her hand. She was fetching water for her family, but the weight and distance were finally too much for her frail body.

And often, people draw from water sources that are not clean and safe. Tainted water transports all kinds of deadly germs and bacteria and is responsible for an unbelievable number of deaths every day. UNICEF estimates that

400 million children have no access to safe drinking water and that 1.5 million children die each year from lack of access to safe drinking water and adequate sanitation. The result is a plethora of diseases. A UNICEF report states that "more than 150 million school-age children are severely affected by waterborne parasites like roundworm, whipworm, and hookworm. These children commonly carry up to 1000 parasites at a time, causing anemia, stunted growth, and other debilitating conditions."[2] These health conditions also affect the ability of students to perform well in school and undermine their chance to get ahead. More than half of all schools worldwide lack safe water and sanitation.

One African leader told me through tears, "These desperate people, on a daily basis, have to decide how they're going to win the battle against poverty, famine, and disease. This is an urgent hour. I believe in long-term economic development, but we can't tell these people we'll build a boat to save them and hope that it gets to them before they drown."

Water Solutions

The good news is that we have the ability to help many of these villages combat droughts and prevent water-related disease through proven water interventions. The most precious natural resource is water, and compassion revolutionaries around the world are working to find ways to bring safe, clean water to communities that need it. Here are three examples of what can be done, simply and effectively.

First, we can help drill wells to tap into water sources deep in the earth. Many people die trying to dig their own wells. Lowered by ropes, they dig by hand, only to have the walls cave in on them. Others have died from methane gases in the wells. And even when people find water, they have no guarantee it will be fit for consumption. The Oasis Project is a leading organization at work on the problem of providing safe and accessible water throughout the African continent. They have many success stories, like the village of Mwanabaya in Tanzania, a village of 2000 inhabitants whose lives were bettered through the drilling of a well. Now, instead of walking miles to retrieve potentially dangerous water, the townspeople of Mwanabaya can bring their buckets to the town pump and get all they need.

Ron Hanson, a field representative for the Oasis Project, reported, "I visited the well and drank the water. It is beautiful, sweet, and clear water, and the pump is easy for the women and children to use." The well can be seen from the door of the church that helped make the well possible and whose pastor watches with joy as the people come to the well to get water. His hope is that the gift of potable water will be a testimony to the caring of the church and lead many to discover Jesus, who promises to provide living water.

Clean water for drinking and irrigation.

Second, we can provide water purification packets. In communities where we can't drill a well, we can help harvest water with guttering cisterns and then make sure it's clean and safe to drink by using purification packets. These little packets, about half the size of a credit card, are filled with a chemical powder that kills harmful bacteria and viruses. Within 30 minutes, previously unsafe water is crystal clear and safe to drink. Procter and Gamble gave Convoy of Hope a gift of $50,000 for the purchase of more than one million packets of PUR water purifier. We were able to distribute these throughout the world in impoverished or disaster-ravaged areas. We have had many corporate partners in our endeavors, and this is a good example of how business and charity can work together.

Third, we can provide water filtration systems. Lives can be saved through the installation of bio-sand filtration units that use local materials to filter the water. With no filters to change, there is no upkeep cost to these units. Each unit can provide enough clean water for an entire family to have safe water every day. How much does such a unit cost? Only about $30. Just think, a one-time investment of only $30 can change the life of an entire family and help them avoid sickness and disease. As we like to say at Convoy of Hope, you can provide a lifetime of clean water to a third world family for about the cost of going out to dinner.

WHAT CAN I DO? SOME PRACTICAL WAYS TO MAKE A DIFFERENCE...

- Indentify and implement three strategies for conserving water in your home.

- Provide financial support for organizations that provide water solutions (see appendix 3 for recommended compassion organizations).

- Conduct a demonstration of a water purification system at your church, job, or school.

It Was a Celebration!

When I first met Wachira Karani, I was immediately impressed with his humility and his dream of helping children throughout Kenya, Somalia, and Ethiopia. His smile gave way to a determined expression: "I was an orphan living on the streets and left to die, and someone rescued me. I have got to save these children before they die of hunger or disease, or waste away sniffing glue." (The glue sniffing is usually related to trying to mask the pain of hunger and thirst.) As a pastor, Wachira had already planted 43 churches, including his own, which more than 700 people attend. The church grounds include a school and a group home for orphans.

I stood with Wachira on a barren piece of land that his church had purchased, and he pointed in multiple directions, showing me where he planned to locate a school that would hold 1500 children. "Over there we will build another group home for orphans, and there a farm and stalls for livestock." Then without warning, he bent to his knees and pointed straight down to the ground and said, "Mr. Dave, I can do all of this if I just had a well right here to supply us with water."

I knelt down beside him and made eye contact. "Pastor, Convoy of Hope will raise the funds to drill this well." We hugged and prayed that God would bring a spring of resources for this worthy project. I returned home and contacted a few pastor friends: Daniel McNaughton of Spring Valley Community Church in Royersford, Pennsylvania, and Michael Jackson of New Life Church in Janesville, Wisconsin. Together they donated the funds for the well and a water pump. Then we prayed that an ample water source could be found on the land.

Pastor Karani standing next to his new well.

News of the project spread throughout the community, so when the rig arrived to drill, so did the crowds. As people prayed and looked on with anticipation, the rig carved through the compacted dirt in a quest for the world's most precious resource. Then, at 164 meters, the miracle of life happened as the drilling unit met a wonderful underground riverbed, and out came clean, fresh water.

Months later I stood with pastor Karani at the spout of the new well. His eyes glistened with excitement as he told me about the day "the water came forth and people arrived from everywhere with plastic containers. The line of people was all the way down the street!" He exclaimed, "It was a celebration like I have never seen!"

"WHY ARE THEY DOING THIS?"
Homes for Homeless Families

When you hear the word *homeless*, what picture comes into your mind? If you are like most people, you'll probably imagine a scruffy bearded man who smells bad and stands on the street corner with a sign, trying to get money that you suspect he will use to buy liquor. Or maybe you think of a young drug addict who sleeps curled up on a park bench and shoplifts to feed his habit. Or perhaps it is a middle-aged woman with a wild and frightening look in her eyes who mutters nonsense and occasionally yells obscenities at passers-by.

We tend to think of the homeless in this way because this is the segment of the homeless population that is most visible and most unavoidable as we go about our daily activities. If this is your impression of homelessness, you are not alone. But the largely hidden segment of the homeless population is made up of families, and the number of homeless children and their parents here in the United States is disturbingly high.

One survey revealed that 53 percent of Americans believe that single adults are more likely to experience homelessness, and only 17 percent believe that families with children were more likely to be without a home.[1] Yet, the truth is that families with young children account for an appalling 50 percent of the nation's homeless.

These families are largely hidden out of sight—sleeping in their cars, abandoned buildings, emergency shelters, or substandard hotels. They don't draw much attention to themselves, and they often try to retain their dignity and some small sense of normalcy for their children. They scrape and save and sacrifice, but they can't seem to get ahead. They float from location to location, looking for work of any sort, and their children's educational development is disrupted by their nomadic lifestyle. When Dad or Mom try to find a job, they will frequently find doors shut when they cannot give an address of residency or are not able to shower, shave, and put on good clothes for an interview.

Those who may suffer most in the wake of this vagabond existence are the children, emotionally bruised from the trauma of roving from place to place and the embarrassment of not having someplace to come home to. They grow up with little security, and in spite of their resilience, these kids tend to show visible signs of their stressful lifestyle, such as depression, deep-seated fears, anxiety, and even high blood pressure. If they are able to attend school, they usually perform below average. I have met a lot of these kids at various Convoy of Hope outreaches and can usually spot them by their unkempt appearance, worn-out countenance, and social reticence. They desire a normal life more than anything, but many of them have lost hope for that. At one of our Christmas outreaches, I asked a young homeless boy what he wanted for Christmas. He just looked up at me with weary yet hopeful eyes and said, "To stay in a home."

Many situations can render a family homeless. Sometimes the family unit is fractured, and the primary breadwinner may disappear. Other times, substance abuse drains the family economy of what little money they might otherwise have. Sometimes parents lack the life skills needed to find and sustain a job. At other times, catastrophe strikes. Families may be displaced by natural disasters, such as devastating floods, hurricanes, and fires. The money-earning member of the family may die, or a job may fall victim to a struggling economy.

Any of these things can leave a family temporarily without housing. And if they do not have a supportive network of family or friends or a caring church, they have no one to lean on for assistance. Or perhaps they stayed with family for a period of time but for various reasons have worn out their welcome. Most of the residents of temporary shelters come after stays with extended families or friends.

A global economic crisis and the resulting foreclosures placed another population group at risk that belies the usual stereotypes of homelessness.

People who never would have dreamed of being out on the street find themselves there when they are unable to pay for housing and consequently lose their homes. The overriding characteristic of homeless families is their extreme poverty. But on top of the three million homeless in America, an additional five million poor spend more than half of their income on housing, leaving them always just on the cusp of homelessness. They would be quick to tell you that with one missed paycheck or a major medical emergency, the mounting bills would push them over the edge into homelessness.

A note also needs to be made about the high number of young people ages 16 to 24 who are homeless. They may comprise as much as 12 percent of the homeless population. Many of these are kids who have run away from home or have been thrown out by their parents. Equally troubling, about 25 percent of the youth who "graduate" out of foster care when they come of age end up homeless in two to four years.

Homeless Shelters

Homeless shelters provide one temporary solution. These are emergency shelters put together to provide immediate short-term relief for families. Usually they involve a sleeping situation without privacy, as many families sleep (or try to sleep) in a single large room. They are frequently only open in the evenings, and often only in the winter months. They are not ideal by any means, but they can be a helpful transition for a family in need, providing for the basic need of a warm, dry, safe place to sleep.

Most cities face the challenge of simply not having adequate shelter space or affordable housing to meet the growing need, leaving many homeless persons with no choice but to live in public spaces. During the past 25 years, our nation has gone from having a surplus of affordable housing units to having a serious deficit of them. In 1971 there were 300,000 more affordable units than there were low-income families who needed them. Today, for every 100 low-income families who need housing, only 75 affordable units are available. My friends who work with temporary shelters tell me that their phones have not stopped ringing with requests and that due to limited capacity, they have to turn homeless families away. That is heartbreaking.

Louis Gill is director of the Bakersfield Homeless Center in Bakersfield, California. He doesn't want to turn anyone away, so he has laid cots and mattresses between the 174 beds in the shelter. Economic woes brought a rush of homeless families to his doors, and he is determined to figure out ways to care for them. "Last year," he says, "we saw a 34 percent increase in homeless families and a 24 percent increase in homeless children." He is determined to try to help these needy families, and the good work he is doing was highlighted in an article published in the *Washington Post*:

> "In a just society, a child should not have to sleep outside or in a car." Gill is a frontline witness to the change in the makeup of the country's homeless. The stereotype of a homeless person as a single man no longer applies. A resident of the Bakersfield center is far more likely to be a young mother with a good, solid job and a mortgage that she just couldn't pay. "They're like folks you know and that you've worked with," Gill said. "Maybe the work's not there right now. Maybe they got behind on their payments. But the idea of a typical homeless person has changed. We're seeing individuals come in that have never had to access the safety net before." Government figures support Gill's experience. The ravages of the recession, including a surge in foreclosures and unemployment approaching 10 percent, have driven thousands of families onto the streets.[2]

Hence the need for churches to step into the gap. I encourage congregations to join together and offer shelter services to the community, especially since most church buildings are only in use a handful of hours every week. Why not partner with other churches in rotation so that once every couple of months your church can provide a place for moms, dads, and their children to sleep? You'll find most of the needy families very grateful and a pleasure to serve.

Habitat for Humanity

The long-term need, though, is not just for temporary shelters, but for affordable housing. Temporary housing should be just that—temporary. People need a better long-term solution. One organization at the forefront of providing affordable homes is Habitat for Humanity. In 1976, Millard and Linda Fuller founded this Christian organization to help provide quality homes for those in need. Now, more than 30 years later, 300,000 homes have been built around the world, providing more than 1.5 million people safe, affordable, good-quality housing.

Habitat for Humanity achieves its goals by an impressive system that includes donated materials, volunteers, and self-empowerment. The new home owners are expected to work hundreds of hours themselves to help construct their homes. Habitat calls this "sweat equity." The homes are built in good areas and, though not luxurious, are attractive and fit well in their neighborhoods. Families that purchase Habitat homes pay very reasonable monthly mortgages because usually they are mostly paying for the land. The monies earned by Habitat go right back into helping build more homes. I talked with Jonathan Reckford, CEO of Habitat for Humanity International, about what they do and why they do it:

Habitat for Humanity.

DAVE: Why are you personally involved in providing shelter?

JONATHAN: I was drawn to Habitat for two important reasons. First, I believe that a safe, decent, and affordable home is the foundation for a better life for every family. Second, the way Habitat engages volunteers to partner with families in need transforms everyone involved in the process. Because families put in sweat equity and pay an affordable no-profit mortgage, they are given the chance to pull themselves up. I had the chance to see that transformation firsthand as a volunteer back in the early '90s and have been a fan of Habitat ever since. Extensive data indicate that stable, affordable housing is central to education, health, employment, and economic development.

DAVE: What is the mission of Habitat for Humanity?

JONATHAN: As a Christian housing ministry, the mission of Habitat for Humanity International is to eliminate poverty housing and homelessness from the face of the earth by building adequate and basic housing. We partner with people of all backgrounds, races, and religions to build houses together in partnership with families in need, and we seek to put shelter on the hearts and minds of people in such a powerful way that poverty housing and homelessness become socially, politically, and religiously unacceptable in our world.

DAVE: How does it work? How do you partner with the community and the family to secure the land, build the home, and then pay for it?

JONATHAN: Through volunteer labor and donations of money and materials, Habitat builds and rehabilitates simple, decent houses alongside home-owner (partner) families. Families in need of decent shelter apply to local Habitat groups called affiliates. The affiliate's family selection committee chooses home owners based on their level of need, their willingness to become partners in the program, and their ability to repay the loan. Every affiliate follows a nondiscriminatory policy of family selection. Habitat is not a giveaway program. In addition to a down payment and monthly mortgage payments, home owners invest hundreds of hours of their own labor into building their Habitat house and the houses of others. Habitat houses are sold to partner families at no profit and financed with affordable loans. The home owners' monthly mortgage payments are used to build more Habitat houses.

DAVE: Why is it important to build collaborations around providing shelter for the poor? What is your strategy?

JONATHAN: Habitat for Humanity cannot be the sole answer to the problem of affordable housing around the world. It is going to take many partners working together on a large scale and in local communities to develop housing solutions. Together, we can accomplish more than each of us can do alone.

DAVE: How can someone volunteer to participate in Habitat for Humanity?

JONATHAN: Much of our work is done through local groups called affiliates. Using the search engine on our website, www.habitat.org, you can locate the affiliate nearest you and talk with the leaders there about volunteering to build or repair a home, about serving on a committee, about donating funds or services, or advocating for just housing policy and more. If you would prefer to join a team that is working in a location in another part of the world, you may wish to join a Global Village team. Check out the Web page for teams that are forming to go to a location that interests you.

The Challenge for the Church

This model of providing homes has a number of advantages over government subsidized housing, which is very often low quality and in the worst parts of the city. I asked a former government official about their strategy for providing the poor with livable housing.

"Well," he said, "we hide them."

"Hide them? What do you mean?" I asked

"The taxpayers don't want to live near—or drive by—ugly housing and reminders of poverty in their community. So we hide them."

Although I am troubled by this strategy, I at least appreciate his transparency. After decades of failed social policy, we are finally realizing that "isolating people in poverty compounds is healthy neither for the poor nor for those who would avoid them."[3] Such clusters of low-income housing are often unsafe, they are eyesores, and they are breeding grounds for crime and social turmoil. It is time we reconsidered this failed strategy.

Studies show that mixed-income housing areas, which blend middle-class and poor families, are the strongest deterrents against homelessness and are very positive for the community. Placing a displaced family in a positive environment does more than just put a roof over their head. It also affords them a sense of dignity—the dignity of home ownership in a good neighborhood. It creates stability and security for the children. It also increases the job prospects for the adults in the family and increases the likelihood that the family will build ties to a local church.

Churches must decide that the current plague of homelessness is not acceptable. Compassion revolutionaries need to support housing programs that build dignity as well as homes, and they ought to consider ways that their church can help provide temporary shelter options and offer people a hand up toward home ownership.

WHAT CAN I DO? SOME PRACTICAL WAYS TO MAKE A DIFFERENCE...

- Volunteer at a homeless shelter.

- Develop a ministry at your church for homeless families.

- Invite a homeless family into your home until they can get on their feet.

- Volunteer at the local affiliate for Habitat for Humanity to help build a home for a family .

The Dream Home

Let me close with the story of one homeless boy and how a church reached out to his family.

Prior to his untimely death, the father of this young man had purchased a fixer-upper home in one city and a vacant lot at the end of a dirt road in a nearby town. While they were working out the details of moving and remodeling their "dream home," the family was living in an inexpensive hotel room. When a reckless car skidded across a divide and collided with the father's car, he was killed, and the dream of a home for the rest of the family appeared likely to die as well. Without any resources, they were poised to lose both the home and the property. In the meantime, they were literally homeless.

But those close to the deceased father knew how much he loved that home and dreamed of it sitting on that barren land he had purchased.

One Saturday the homeless boy, his mother, and his siblings were asked by a church member to meet him at the vacant lot. Approaching the vacant lot the young boy thought, *Why would we visit a weed-infested piece of dirt?* They drove down the dirt road, which sloped into a cul-de-sac, expecting to see a vacant lot. Instead, sitting proudly in its place, was their father's dream home. Cars dotted the shoulder all along the road, and people were walking around with shovels, hammers, paintbrushes, plants, and carpet.

"What's going on?" the boy asked.

As he walked closer to the house, he saw all the activity of a giant anthill, with men busy painting the exterior, installing new windows, and planting bushes and trees. Inside the home was the unmistakable smell of new carpet. A group of women were hanging curtains, arranging new furniture, and guiding movers as they installed appliances.

The dream home.

Puzzled and surprised by the day's events, the boy walked out the back door and around to the front, trying to digest what was happening. Standing some distance from the house, he stared at the workers and realized that he recognized most of them. Many were from his dad's church, and others were from another fellowship in a neighboring city.

Why are they doing this? the boy asked himself in utter disbelief. *Why are they helping my family? Why are they helping us? We can never pay them back.*

But he was struck by how happy the volunteers looked.

That day changed the heart of that little boy and transformed his desperate family's life. The volunteers' compassion helped the boy recognize the value he had in God's eyes. The home also provided dignity and stability beyond description for the boy and his homeless family.

Some months later, the man who had originally sold the land to his dad dropped by to pay his respects to the grieving widow. He had recently paved the road and built other homes on the street. With a smile of great satisfaction, he presented the woman a special gift in honor of her deceased husband. It was a wooden sign that would mark the name of the new street. When she read the sign her tears began to flow. The street would be named after her husband and *my* dad—Donaldson Court.

"DAD, LET'S BRING UP THE BEDS"
Foster Care and Adoption

D avid, your mother and I believe it is the right time to open our home to a young boy who has no home." I was sitting on my son's bed and trying to help him understand the decision that his mother and I had made. After much thought and prayer, we both felt that God was leading us to take in a young boy as a foster child. We knew that our decision would have an impact on David, so I was trying to explain why we had decided this and what its impact upon him would be.

"Son," I said gingerly, "to do this, we'll need you to share your room. We can take your double bed down to the basement and bring up the two twin beds."

He looked at me in total disbelief and a bit of panic. "Do you mean I have to share my room with someone I don't even know?"

I searched my mind for a way to help him understand as I looked out his bedroom window. It was a cold, drizzly day. "Look out there," I suggested. "If a young boy was out there and had no home, would you invite him in? If the boy had been passed from home to home, would you be willing to say, 'Come stay with us'?"

David stared out the window and did not respond. I could see the wheels turning in his brain.

"Pray about it and let me know what you think," I said, patting his knee. Standing up, I took another look at the miserable weather outside and went downstairs.

About a half hour went by, and then David came down and found me in the kitchen.

"Dad," he said, "let's bring up the beds."

Wrapping my arms around him, I said, "This earthly father is very proud, but it does not begin to compare with how proud your heavenly Father is right now."

David had to count the cost in terms of inconvenience, the loss of some privacy, and having to step outside his comfort zone. But all these concerns were dwarfed by the realization that he could not say no to a young boy in need. If we are going to consider helping children who need to be adopted or be provided with foster care, we'll have to think through similar issues. I hope that like David, we'll be willing to sacrifice some of our own ease to help others.

According to the Bible, we are all adopted. This is one of Scripture's most beautiful and meaningful images of our relationship with God. The apostle Paul writes, "He predestined us to be adopted as his sons through Jesus Christ, in accordance with his pleasure and will—to the praise of his glorious grace, which he has freely given us in the One he loves" (Ephesians 1:5-6). In the Roman culture in which Paul lived, adoption was a very serious matter.

> Within Roman society...adoption was a legal reality. Under Roman law, an adopted child became a new person. He received a new name, a new identity. Adoptees were legally separated from everything that made up their past, and were given legal rights to all the wealth and fortunes of their new families![1]

Paul reminds us that when God chose us to be His children, He chose us and adopted us as His sons and daughters through Jesus Christ, out of His own pleasure and will! When we enter into relationship with Jesus Christ, we are adopted into the family of God. As in Roman adoption, we are given a new identity and access to the gifts that come from our new Father.

Doesn't it make sense, then, that we who have ourselves experienced the blessings of adoption by God should in turn reach out to those who need to be adopted or sheltered? James defines the quality of our faith by how we care for those without parents. "Pure and genuine religion in the sight of God the Father means caring for orphans and widows in their distress and refusing to let the world corrupt you" (James 1:27 NLT). We were separated from God our Father, alienated because of sin. Yet He found us in our orphan state and adopted us with pleasure. In the same way, when we align our will with God's and make room in our home for someone without a family, we practice "pure and genuine religion." Let that sink in. Our high calling is to lift lowly orphans up in their time of distress.

We can serve family-less children in many ways, but this chapter will highlight two ways that you might want to consider: foster care and adoption. These may not be options for everyone, but I'd like to challenge you to open your heart to the possibility.

Orphans in the USA

When we hear about orphans, we often think of children overseas in orphanages or living on the street in foreign cities. But approximately 500,000 children throughout the United States are in the foster care system, and 127,000 are still waiting for permanent adoptive families.

Ralph Berry is a former Baptist minister who left the pastorate to work with a private foster care agency in Northern Virginia. Here's what he says:

> I see these beautiful kids enter foster care because they have been abused and neglected. For example, we had a boy who slept underneath his bed in the foster home for six months because that is where he slept in his birth home. [It was the safest place for him with all of the domestic violence that went on all hours of the day and night.] We had an eleven-year old who was pregnant with her mom's boyfriend's baby. We had three kids who had never been out of their home in their life. The dad wanted his two little girls back, but not the son. [The two little girls have been groomed by dad to be his paramours.]

It is heartbreaking to think what these kids have been through. When I asked Ralph why people should consider becoming foster parents, he replied, "To change the world one child at a time." He believes this is a powerful ministry that the whole church should embrace. We should be taking the lead when it comes to protecting and caring for these children.

Tear Down the Wall!

In 2004 I was asked by the United States Children's Bureau to host a historic summit between faith-based leaders and state government agency directors for foster care and adoption. The event began with the government workers on one side of a partition and the faith-based leaders on the other. I was scheduled to speak prior to the former Health and Human Services Secretary, Tommy Thompson. I pointed to the partition and looked out over the crowd of more than 800 faith-based leaders. "On the other side of this partition are well-meaning government workers who are trying to find a solution to the plight of more than 500,000 children currently trapped in a well-meaning but cold and impersonal foster care system. On this side of the partition, we are the Christian community, given a mandate to include these children in our families." I quoted what God has said in Psalms: God is "a father to the fatherless," and he "sets the lonely in families" (Psalm 68:5-6). Then, turning toward the partition and the government leaders on the other side, I stole a famous line from Ronald Reagan and declared, "Mr. Secretary, tear down this wall! We want these children!"

Genuine religion is to care for orphans.

Make no mistake about it; these children will not remain in limbo while we make up our minds. Their futures are being determined every day that passes.

The very next morning after making this declaration, I received an urgent message from a government official stating that the homosexual community was mounting a national protest because they were not invited to participate in the summit. If we do not make room for kids without a family, other people who do not share our values are more than willing to snatch them up.

Wanted: Imperfect Parents

Across the nation, I have talked with many Christian adults who would like to become foster parents but have never taken that step because of fear of failure and the unknown. They recognize all too well their imperfections as parents. But perfection is not what is needed. Rather, these kids long for love and caring.

A few years ago the U.S. Children's Bureau produced several very creative commercials to recruit foster and adoptive parents. Their theme was "You don't have to be perfect to be a perfect parent." One of my favorites opens with a father and son playing musical instruments in their garage. The boy is on the drums and the dad is trying to play the saxophone. A close-up shows the boy grimacing as his dad squeaks up and down the scale, trying to find the right key. Then both the father and son glance at each other, smiling ear to ear, as you hear the voiceover, "You don't have to be perfect to be a perfect parent."

Another commercial begins with two boys playing basketball outside their home. One boy shoots the ball, and it gets stuck between the rim and the backboard. The two boys moan as they stare up at the ball, thinking that their game is ruined. Just then a mom enters the scene carrying a broom. She points the handle toward the basketball and dislodges it, much to the boys' glee. Again you hear the voiceover, "You don't have to be perfect to be a perfect parent." What these children need most is simply the presence of a caring adult. And as someone has said, love is spelled T-I-M-E.

What Do You Want with That?

Bob and Cheryl Reccord tell an amazing story about adoption in their book *Launching Your Kids for Life*. It illustrates so well the impact you can make in children's lives when you invite them into yours through foster parenting or adoption:

> Several years ago, in the picturesque tidewater basin of the Virginia coast, three young boys were born in stair-step fashion. In a period

of three years, all three had stepped into this brave new world. But not every child who steps into the world finds a pleasant or easy reception awaiting him. For these three, the journey ahead would be anything but smooth sailing.

The father, who was involved in the military, was an alcoholic. While some people become humorous when they have too much to drink, others take on a less than pleasant demeanor. This father happened to be in the latter category. Soon after the third son was born, the mother was stricken with cancer. Life became much more than she could handle. She was striving to take care of three children all under the age of three, she was battling cancer, and she was trying to cope with an alcoholic husband and father to her children. By the time her youngest was eleven months old, she gave up the fight and died.

The father now found himself responsible not only for a military career, but also for raising three small children. Sometimes he was up to the task, sometimes not. The responsibility and demands were more than he wanted to face. Compared to raising three preschoolers, the military was a breeze!

Also, the responsibilities got in the way of his enjoying a good drink now and then…or more often. When he got tired of the boys, he would throw them out to another home—any home—that would take them off his hands and give him a break for a while. When he needed to feel good about himself, or to claim financial aid for his dependent children, he would grab them back. Thus the cycle began: he would hand off the kids to others to get some breathing room, then he would drag the kids back and force himself into the role of a parent.

The cycle repeated until finally, having had all the fun he could stand, he threw the boys out for what was the last time. The three were passed from hand to hand and house to house, all the way from Virginia to southern Illinois, where they found themselves deposited in another home willing to take them in—at least for a short while.

Meantime, a young couple in southern Illinois had tried to have children but had suffered through three miscarriages and one stillbirth. The stillbirth had been traumatic because the baby had been discovered dead in the mother's womb. Physicians had not diagnosed it early enough, and so peritonitis had set in, which poisoned the womb of the mother. The doctors had done well to pull her through the trauma, but in the end they told her there was no hope for any more children in the future.

Hearing of the little fellows' plight, the young couple found their way to the home where the youngsters had been staying. They knocked on the front door. "We understand you have some little boys here who are in need of a home. We thought we'd come and see if we could be of any help." The gruff lady who opened the door quickly indicated that the two older boys had been taken by a couple, leaving only the youngest. "The brat's in the back! Take a look if you want to...it's up to you." With that she wheeled around and walked away.

Making their way through the house, they came to a back bedroom where the little guy was playing. It was obvious he hadn't been washed in days. He was sitting in diapers that had long since needed changing.

What was worse, the little fellow was covered with a disease called impetigo, which creates body sores that ooze with a puslike discharge. In other words, the boy was a ghastly mess.

Not to be deterred, the young wife gathered him up in her arms with no thought to the stains that immediately appeared on her new dress. "We'll take him! We'll take him!" she said. Shrugging her shoulders, the gruff home owner said, "Do what you like." And she let them out of the house.

They arrived at the local doctor's office and set the little boy on the examining table. When the doctor entered the room and saw the dirty and diseased child, the comment that came rolling out of his mouth before he could catch it was, "My God! What do you want with that?" Some people discount anyone who doesn't have beauty, brains, or bucks. This doctor was no exception.

But the young wife answered, "We're willing to take him because, if somebody like us doesn't, he'll never have the chance to become what God created him to be."[2]

Does this sound like the beginning of a novel? Something you might see in a movie? Well, it is a true story. You've just read the beginning of Bob's own life.

The story doesn't end there. Neither of Bob's adoptive parents had finished high school. Both of them had challenging upbringings. But they loved him and shared the immensity of God's love with him. Bob's adopted mom encouraged Bob with thoughts like these:

"God has a special plan for you, and He's giving us the joy of being a part of it."

"God created you for a purpose, and we're committed to helping you find it."

"God knew your future even before you were born, and He's got a plan for you to fulfill!"

And when Bob became impatient, his mother would say, "Be patient, because God's not finished with you yet!"

Bob applied these lessons well. As the late Paul Harvey would say, here is "the rest of the story." This little boy that nobody wanted went on to become a successful pastor, a prolific speaker and writer, adviser to world leaders, and president of the North American Missions Board for the Southern Baptist denomination. He now directs a ministry called Made to Count, which inspires people to discover their calling in life and to effectively develop and exercise their passion for God and His mission. Only God knows how our love and compassion can change a life and how that life will be used— perhaps like Dr. Bob Reccord's—to change the world.

Making Room

I had the privilege of working alongside Terry Meeuwsen when I served at Operation Blessing for the Christian Broadcasting Network. Since 1993, Terry has been a cohost of CBN's *The 700 Club*. She also cohosts *Living the Life* and is director of Orphan's Promise. She is a busy woman. But more important to her, she is the mother of seven children, five of whom are adopted. Her latest book, *The God Adventure*, shares the story of her family's adoption of three sisters from Ukraine. She talks about how important God's leading is in the decision to adopt: "As individuals and as families we must always ask the Lord for vision and direction before doing anything. James 4:2 says, 'You do not have because you do not ask.'"[3]

Adopting a child, whether a child from the U.S. or a child from another country, is a big step, but do not let the fear of the unknown keep you from exploring further. Two of the best resources for answers to questions about adoption are Bethany Christian Services and Focus on the Family.

Bethany Christian Services has found loving homes for more than 25,000 children since 1944 when it first began guiding adoptive parents through the exciting journey of international adoption. Christian musician Steven Curtis Chapman and his wife, Mary Beth, are among the thousands of couples who have adopted through Bethany. More information is available at www.bethany.org.

Focus on the Family has been at the vanguard in raising the awareness of the plight of orphans worldwide and challenging Christians to become "forever families" to these children. You might also want to refer to appendix 2 of this book: "Frequently Asked Questions About Foster Care and Adoption."

It won't always be easy, and compassion is rarely convenient, but countless foster care and adoptive parents will quickly tell you that your marriage, children, and home will be enriched by practicing "pure religion" that pleases God (James 1:27).

WHAT CAN I DO? SOME PRACTICAL WAYS TO MAKE A DIFFERENCE...

- Pray about becoming a foster or adoptive parent.
- Read the frequently asked questions in appendix 2.
- Attend an orientation hosted by a local foster care agency to learn about becoming a foster parent.
- Work with a local agency to become a "respite" parent who takes in a foster child for a weekend to give the foster parents a break.
- For adoption information, contact Bethany Christian Services.

He Makes All Things New

During our training to become foster parents, our instructor handed each of the prospective parents, including my wife and me, a Styrofoam cup. He asked us to draw a picture of what we believed our foster child would look like. I traced the face of a young boy on the side of the cup, and others drew pictures of their own ideas about their soon-to-be foster children. When we were done, we all proudly held up our cups for the others in the class to see.

To our surprise, the instructor told us to tear our cup into pieces. I was puzzled, but I followed the odd request until a pile of Styrofoam pieces filled my hand. The instructor walked over to me and asked me to hand him the pieces. He looked at the pieces for a moment and then handed them back to me and said, "This is the foster care system. Here is your child. Now fix him."

I stared down at the broken pieces that represented my broken foster child. The instructor handed us rolls of tape to form the pieces back into a cup again.

"You might be able to restore the cup," he explained as we worked, "but the scars will always be there."

Suddenly I had an idea. I grabbed a new cup, drew the same picture of the boy on the side, and then placed the repaired cup inside the new one.

"What are you doing?" a lady next to me asked.

Holding up the new cup I declared, "My God, who loves this child even more than I do, can remove the scars and make him new!"

None of us will be perfect parents. We may think our home is unsuitable for a lonely child. We might say this is not the right time or stage of life to include a child. There are plenty of reasons not to become a foster or adoptive parent. But perhaps there is one reason to say yes—maybe God is telling you it is time. You see, the only way God can fulfill His promise to be a father to the fatherless is through you and me. Are you the answer to one of the 500,000 children praying to be accepted into a loving family? Will you open your heart and home and say, *Yes, God, I will bring up the bed*?

Sometimes the compassion revolution begins very close to home—in fact, sometimes it might even begin *in* our home.

"TODAY IS A GOOD DAY"
Reaching Out to the Cities

When our Convoy of Hope trucks come rolling into town for one of the community outreaches, we come bringing hope and help under the banner of a compassionate God and His church. Outreaches take place at stadiums, parks, or other large venues and include hot meals, medical and dental screening, haircuts, bags of groceries, job placement services, counseling, and a connection to local churches and community organizations. And we do it all in an atmosphere that is both dignified and fun! Entertainment is even available, as well as a special Kid's Zone with activities for the little ones. All of this is provided free.

Partnering with local organizations, churches, businesses, and government agencies, we design these outreaches to meet both the practical and the spiritual needs of the community. And it isn't just about one-time assistance either. One of the goals of each outreach is to let our guests know where and how they can get the ongoing, long-term support, resources, and encouragement they need.

At a Convoy of Hope outreach in Baltimore, I stood at an exit as the guests prepared to leave. We had enjoyed a gratifying day. But more importantly, we wanted to make sure the guests enjoyed themselves and received the help they needed. So as people left, I asked many of them if they did. We hoped to catch their responses on film.

I approached a woman who was there with her daughter and grandchild, and I held out the microphone, "Did you enjoy yourself today?"

She pulled her granddaughter close to her side, looked down at her for a moment and softly said, "Today was a good day." Then she looked at me and I saw tears begin to form in the corners of her eyes. "You know, I've been going through a lot..." Her voice broke and trailed off. She began to weep.

It took a few moments before she could continue. "But today..." she said, "today is a good day." Now tears were streaming down my cheeks while I tried to keep the microphone steady. "I met the pastor, and he invited me to church. I told him I didn't have anything nice to wear, but he said, 'That's okay, God doesn't look at the outside, but the inside.'" And then she began to cry again.

I could no longer treat this as an interview. Tucking away the microphone, I wrapped my arms around her. "Do you realize how precious you are to Jesus?" I asked, my own voice catching in my throat. "He loves you so much...and so do we."

A smile formed on her lips.

"Today is a good day!" she insisted. "I know I'm going to be all right. Today is a good day!"

This lovely woman did not feel worthy to enter a church because of her poverty. Until the day of the outreach, there was no one in her life to tell her what really mattered to Jesus. How many people are still outside the church family, waiting to hear this message? Do the racial and socioeconomic divides keep us from being aware of each other and helping each other?

Guests of Honor

In the parable of the Good Samaritan (Luke 10:29-37), Jesus tells the story of an unfortunate man left alongside a road, hurt and helpless after a robbery and beating. He is ignored by a priest and a Levite who pass by until someone finally comes along who has compassion on him and offers him practical help. Risking the possibility that he himself could be attacked if the robbers are still lurking nearby, and allowing his own plans and priorities to be disrupted, the Good Samaritan reaches out, getting personally involved with the victim and his problems. He spent time and money (and had to muster some courage) to make a difference in the life of the poor unfortunate man.

Like the Good Samaritan, we have learned the importance of getting personally involved at our outreaches, treating those who come for help not as objects of pity, but as honored guests. We take pride in our "Honored Guest" principle. Michael Redmon, vice president of outreach for Convoy of Hope, set our goal for every outreach: to value, respect, and treat as a guest of honor every person who receives help. Every aspect of the outreach is based on this principle. On the day of the outreach, all areas of service demonstrate this principle in action—unconditionally loving and accepting each guest without regard to age, race, physical appearance, or spiritual condition. When we host guests of honor, we don't see "us and them." Rather, we are a community, joining together to have a great day of giving and receiving.

This attitude makes a difference. It creates an atmosphere of love and hope. An organizer at one of our events thanked a police officer for the help the police department provided during the event. "You don't understand," said the officer. "This is our beat. We see this neighborhood every day, and we have never experienced this kind of peace. This place, from one side of the park to the other, is usually filled with all kinds of crime and violence. It was such a pleasure to see everyone getting along for once."

Convoy of Hope outreach.

That is our goal in the community outreaches—not only to meet immediate practical needs but also to plant seeds of the peace and love of Christ so that hope may blossom in some of the darkest places in our world.

Jesus and a Job

Some exciting things happen at these events. I've coordinated and participated in hundreds of these outreaches, and I love visiting the different outreach tents, which provide such services as haircuts and manicures, family photographs, and health screenings. I especially enjoy seeing the job fair area, where experts help guests craft résumés and sometimes even do job interviews right on the spot. What a thrill to meet a guest who arrives jobless but leaves with a good prospect or even employment.

The cliché "All they need is Jesus" does not take into consideration the millions in America and around the world who need both Jesus and a job! Most of the solutions to the world's systemic problems can be reduced to the need for skill development and employment.

How can I ever forget Jim, who attended a Convoy of Hope outreach looking for a job. He stood beside his son, gazing dejectedly at the ground. Even from a distance, his beaten-down demeanor caught my eye as I mingled with the line of people waiting to enter the outreach.

"Are there going to be clowns and balloons?" his son asked me as I drew near.

"Yes, of course, and hot dogs, games, bouncing gyms, and even prizes," I told him.

I offered my hand to the father. "My name is Dave. I want to thank you for coming today."

He shook my hand and replied with little emotion, "I'm Jim."

"Jim, how long have you lived in the area?"

"A few years," he muttered. Then he looked me in the eye and blurted out, "I've tried to find work, but it seems nobody wants me."

Jim's son had walked away a pace or two.

"I don't want my boy to think his dad's a bum," he said urgently. "I don't want him to grow up to be like me either."

The pain in his face and voice was pushing me toward tears. "We have people here today who will help you put together a good résumé," I said. "Employers are looking for someone just like you who is eager to work."

A few days later I visited Jim and his son at their home. They lived in public housing that was cold, dark, and cramped. After several knocks, the door magically swung open.

"Who is it?" came a voice from the back of the room.

"It's Dave from the outreach," I replied, hoping he would remember me.

"C'mon in, Dave."

As I walked past the open door, I noticed it was his little boy who had opened the door. He jumped up for a high five.

Jim was sitting at the kitchen table, completing some forms. There was a new energy about him. "Do you know what these are?" he asked with a smile. "These are papers I need to finish for my new job."

I reached out my hand to congratulate him, and he grasped it with confidence.

"Dave," he said, almost shouting with joy, "thank you! At that thing you guys put on last Saturday...well, I found Jesus and a job!"

David Beckman, president of Bread for the World and a foremost advocate for the poor, says, "The best solution to hunger is a decent job. Some people are elderly, disabled or, for other reasons, cannot work. They need safety-net programs. But when poor people are asked what they most need, they ask for a stable, well-paying job or an educational opportunity that will lead to a good job."[1]

Red, Yellow, Black, and White

Among other things, Convoy outreaches in American cities expose the reality that the darkest places in the world may not be very far away from your own front door. The level of hopelessness and despair of many who live within our cities would probably come as a surprise to many, whose picture of poverty is of unfortunate people living on the other side of the world in hunger and squalid conditions. Well, a similar mixture of hunger, squalor, and hopelessness can be found right here in the United States, though it might be hidden away in parts of our cities where most of us rarely go.

A couple of decades ago we began to hear about the "white flight" of middle-class Caucasians relocating from the inner cities to the suburbs. But now city centers are being reclaimed for business, and downtowns are reviving. City planners have worked to make city centers places for trendy shops, restaurants, and "river walks." "Young professionals, as well as empty nesters, are flooding into our cities, buying up lofts and condos and dilapidated historic residences, opening avant-garde artist studios and gourmet eateries."[2] The poor are being shifted to a space between the downtown areas and the suburbs. Some have called this "the donut effect."

Of course, the potential downside to businesses and professionals migrating to the inner cities is the "disinvestment" that can occur in the areas they leave behind. One Christian social worker put it this way: "Homeowners move away, landlords defer maintenance, the quality of life declines, property values depreciate, legitimate businesses leave and illegitimate enterprise fills the void."[3] This disinvestment and decrease in incomes will result in fewer tax dollars for the government to invest in social services and infrastructure.

But this void can be seen as an opportunity for churches to become centers of hope in these areas where the poor are relocating. These newly diverse areas have become a multiethnic field that is ripe for harvest.

Wendel Cover, the International pastor.

The church I attend, Word of Life International, was once a traditional Anglo congregation in a suburb of Washington DC. But the demographic changes we discussed above began to alter our look and then our outlook.

Instead of being afraid of the changes, our pastor, Wendel Cover, welcomed them…literally. He placed a message on the church marquee that read, "All Nationalities Welcome." It was a public welcome mat that continues to attract new members from all kinds of ethnic backgrounds and faith traditions. Now our church has become a melting pot of people representing more than 100 nationalities. As Pastor Cover likes to say, "Each Sunday I can travel around the world without leaving home!" We used to just be called Word of Life, but we added *International* to celebrate the cultural transformation in our church family. We now have an international school, a beautiful mosaic representing our mission to disciple children who are red, yellow, black, and white. A typical Sunday service includes international choirs that wear their native dress and sing in their native language. We are a miniature portrait of God's rainbow.

Broken Windows and Repaired Communities

New York City provides a good example of the demographic changes taking place around the nation. In the 1980s, New York City was a virtual combat zone of filth and violence. By the end of that decade, 20,000 felonies were on the books. Tourism, long an important New York industry, was slipping due to American and European visitors' fears that they might become the next crime victims. Then, from a high in 1990, things began to shift, and the crime rate began to decline. Murders dropped by two-thirds and felonies by half.

Experts credit the reverse in crime to counteracting what has come to be known as the broken-window theory. Malcolm Gladwell explains: "If a window is broken and left unrepaired, people walking by will conclude that no one is in charge. Soon, more windows will be broken, and the state of anarchy will spread from the building to the street on which it faces, sending a signal that anything goes." In other words, crime and decay are contagious.

I experienced this for myself when I visited an inner-city park and saw a small pile of trash near the basketball court. A week later I visited the same site and the pile had grown five times its size. As an experiment I gathered about half of the trash and threw it in a nearby garbage can. The other half I moved to a new location. Sure enough, after just one week, the pile had more than doubled in size! People follow the example of others, for good and for bad.

Such seemingly minor problems as littering, graffiti, and panhandling are all viewed by the community as broken windows. They send the message that no one cares, so they lure more serious crimes. When Rudolph Guliani became mayor of New York City in 1994, he applied the broken-window theory to the city at large, enforcing the laws against public drunkenness, vandalism, and littering, which were often referred to as "quality of life crimes." This new attention to cleaning up the streets (literally) began to reverse the broken-window epidemic. Now, the streets of New York are much cleaner and much safer than they have been in years.

What if the church applied its own broken-window strategy? What if we cleaned up parks, picked up trash, repaired broken windows, and renovated dilapidated buildings? What if churches offered programs to help people develop life skills that enabled them to raise families, sustain jobs, and rid neighborhoods of substance abuse? What if we established outreaches to teenage girls who are at high risk of becoming unwed mothers? Could acts like these renew our cities, ushering in an epidemic of compassion that others would want to join and be a part of? If we started caring and doing something, many others would likely join us in the effort.

WHAT CAN I DO? SOME PRACTICAL WAYS TO MAKE A DIFFERENCE...

- Participate in a Convoy of Hope outreach (see www.convoyofhope.org for the U.S. outreach schedule).

- Organize a group of volunteers to clean up parks and other public areas.

- Offer to do lawn work, home repairs, or car maintenance for an elderly person.

- Bake some cookies and take them to an elderly person or shut-in.

Restorers of the Streets

Can we embrace a vision similar to that which the prophet Zechariah had for the restoration of the Jewish people to Israel? "This is what the LORD Almighty says: 'Once again men and women of ripe old age will sit in the streets of Jerusalem, each with cane in hand because of his age. The city streets will be filled with boys and girls playing there'" (Zechariah 8:4).

As I am writing this section of this book, I am in Jerusalem. Today as I walked through the streets of the Old City of Jerusalem, I decided to eat in the Jewish quarter. Sitting at my table, I watched with elation and amazement as the elderly sat peacefully on benches, talking and reading. Around them were scores of school children playing games and laughing. If God can accomplish this in a city that has been the stage of countless wars and struggles over the centuries, He can certainly use your church as a tipping point for reversing decay and bringing restoration!

What do our churches need to do if we are to expand our ministries to the impoverished in the cities?

First, we need to do a serious assessment of what the needs are and whether they are being met. Some churches have made the mistake of developing programs without first assessing the actual needs of their city, so they failed to really take aim at the most serious issues. We need to do demographic studies to determine whom we are trying to help: their race, age, income, disabilities, education, level of home ownership, employment, and so on. It might even be a good idea to go door to door, asking the people in our communities what their greatest needs are, what programs currently exist to meet those needs, and where the programs are falling short.

Second, we need to identify what churches, organizations, businesses, and government agencies are already doing. The local United Way or the Department of Health and Human Services might be able to help you get this information. (But keep in mind that the good works of churches are often not officially listed in the directory of services, so you might have to contact churches directly to find out what they are doing.) The point is, duplicating effective programs while neglecting unmet needs makes no sense.

Third, look at whom you have in your congregation that might want to get involved. Consider their abilities, their gifts, and their level of participation. Remember that some people are too shy and retiring to step out and offer or volunteer, but they might be overjoyed to help if you ask them to take a significant role.

Fourth, don't get discouraged if you don't see immediate results. Change takes time—in communities and in individuals. I remember my former church working with one homeless man whom we were trying to help replace his bad habits with good ones. His slow learning curve left me exhausted. On some days I felt like the only tree in a dog kennel! Poverty holds on to its victims pretty stubbornly, and breaking the bondage can take years. But we can cling to the promise found in 2 Corinthians 5:17: "Therefore, if anyone is in Christ, he is a new creation; the old has gone, the new has come!" God is continually working overtime to restore and renew His people.

Fifth, know when to rest and when to quit. Too many well-meaning compassion revolutionaries experience fatigue and burnout from their work with the poor. In a later chapter we'll discuss ways to avoid "compassion fatigue."

Sixth, remember that the deepest need of everyone you serve is for them to have a personal relationship with Jesus Christ. If we are not careful, we can get so involved in meeting the complex and diverse needs of our communities that we leave Jesus on the sidelines. Countless churches and charities have made the mistake of exchanging Jesus for a compassion ministry.

Let's not forget Jesus' words to the church at Ephesus: "I know your deeds, your hard work and your perseverance…You have persevered and have endured hardships for my name, and have not grown weary. Yet I hold this against you: You have forsaken your first love" (Revelation 2:2-4). As we seek to be compassion revolutionaries in our cities, let's remember that the most transforming thing we can do is to introduce people to the original compassion revolutionary, Jesus Christ.

Your church might not be able to stage something as large as one of our Convoy of Hope outreaches, but even the smallest congregation can participate and find other practical ways to offer hope and help to the needy in their community. All it takes is the desire, some creativity, and a little elbow grease. Wouldn't it be great to provide another "good day" for someone who has all too few of them?

14

CORPORATE CITIZENSHIP

O nce upon a time, the corporate heads of most companies had a single mission: "How much money can we make, and how fast can we make it?" But many corporations are beginning to think differently about their role and responsibility in the world. The almighty dollar is still the bottom line for most businesses, but more of today's employers are finding that making a good profit is not enough if they want to keep their employees, investors, suppliers, and customers happy. A new movement, aimed at connecting the demands of Wall Street and Main Street, has sometimes been referred to as "corporate citizenship." Responsibility and the demand for ethical business practices have increasingly come to the fore and begun to create a new corporate culture for many businesses. An important part of this new culture is seeing the value in participating in compassion projects, which are seen as a "social investment." Such involvement is increasingly seen not only as a good business practice but also as the right thing to do.

It's the Right Thing

Corporate involvement in compassion can do more than generate immediate good publicity. It can provide important value for businesses in other ways too. Cary Summers, CEO of the Nehemiah Group, is a former executive for Abercrombie & Fitch, Bass Pro Shops, and the Silver Dollar Corporation. He told me the story about his involvement with helping build a Habitat for Humanity home for a single mom and her kids. Initially he saw that it made good business sense. "Admittedly," Cary says, "it was good public relations for my company to be seen reinvesting back into our community by building a home for a single parent. On my left side, former president Jimmy Carter was hammering nails. On my right was a lady who was going to own the house we were building. This was a nice lady who was trying to do her best to raise her family after a series of bad breaks, including abandonment by her husband."

As Cary worked alongside her, though, he realized that this was so much more than a good photo op. He saw that it was literally life-changing for her! "I will never forget the day when this woman and her children entered their new home—a home she had helped build. It was like a huge Christmas party!" As he told me about it, I saw Cary's face break into a smile. "But I had so much fun, and it was 'the Jesus thing to do.' It's the right thing to do even if it doesn't materialize into a single dime of profit for your company."

Like Cary Summers, many business women and men are discovering the rewards of living their faith through their work. Business and faith should not be considered two entirely different spheres. Billy Graham once said, "I believe one of the next great moves of God is going to be through believers in the marketplace."

Work Is Worship

Work is a central theme in the Bible, with more than 800 references to the value and place of labor. *Avodah* is the transliteration of a Hebrew root word for both *worship* and *work*. Have you ever thought about the close connection of the two actions? The root word of each of them means "to serve." An *oved* is a worker. An *evid* is a slave. *Avdut* is slavery. Work, therefore, involves the act of serving someone. *Avodat Elohim* is service to or worship of the true God. And any act of work is an act of serving. It's a helpful way to think about our vocational lives. They are to be lives of service.

From the very beginning, Adam and Eve were given the mission of tending the Garden and taking care of it (Genesis 2:15). This was their work. And Jesus reminded us that God is continually working: "My Father is always at his work to this very day, and I, too, am working" (John 5:17). Work has the divine stamp of approval because it is part of being created in the image of God. Chuck Colson has pointed out the difference between our modern cultural perspective on work and the biblical perspective: "Much of our culture has a distinctly Greek view of work: We work out of necessity. But, you see, we are made in the image of God, and as such we are made to work—to create, to shape, to bring order out of disorder."[1]

If work is part of our natural DNA as beings created in God's image, then it only makes sense that we worship God through our labor in the marketplace. Jesus was never afraid of hard work or the business environment—after all, He was raised the son of a carpenter! Many might be surprised that 122 of Jesus' 132 public appearances that are recorded in the New Testament took place in the marketplace. When He chose 12 disciples, He chose businessmen rather than clergy. And when He taught the parables, 45 out of 52 had a workplace setting. From a biblical perspective there is no hesitation about mixing business and ministry. That is the lesson that a growing group of business executives are learning.

Many business leaders who are practicing good corporate citizenship are learning they can help the poor in other ways in addition to donating money. They are giving their time and expertise as well, getting personally involved in helping the needy and finding the satisfaction that comes from making a difference. Chuck Bengochea is the CEO of the HoneyBaked Ham Company. But he is also very involved in working with Convoy of Hope as a national spokesperson to the corporate community. In an interview, Chuck talked about his involvement with compassion ministry:

INTERVIEWER: How does your faith influence the way you do business?

CHUCK: I strive to always be aware that I'm a witness for God. One of the things I publicly say in my company all the time is I'm not interested in my legacy being how many hams I sold. But I want my legacy to be how many people I impact. That's what I'm more interested in. How many people did I love with God's love? At the end of the day, no matter how bad my flesh wants to screw things up, I try not to lose sight that I serve God and represent Him. That's a joyful privilege, but it's also a sobering one.

INTERVIEWER: How has being involved with Convoy of Hope changed you?

CHUCK: My natural bent is toward serving and giving, but probably the most visible way it's changed me is it's made me want to do even more.

There's something about people being sold out, like the folks at Convoy. That's changed me.

INTERVIEWER: How is compassion ministry valuable to the church?

CHUCK: It's clear who Jesus spent His time with—the prostitutes, tax collectors, and the sinners. If we aren't willing to do that, then we aren't living out His gospel. And if we're not living out His gospel, then we become irrelevant. It's a hurting world out there. I think we're all too comfortable—in our lifestyles, in what we do, in our comfortable homes. But we have to be jarred out of that. We have to get outside of that and go serve and make ourselves relevant. If you love people well, then you get the privilege and the opportunity to let the Holy Spirit work in their lives.[2]

Becoming Corporate Citizens

Chuck Bengochea and Cary Summers embody what Oswald Chambers taught: "The spiritual manifests itself in a life which knows no division into sacred and secular." These business leaders have effectively integrated their faith and learning into everyday life. Anne Beiler (founder of Auntie Anne's) is another leader who has modeled this balance. She once said to me, "I am called to the business world. I shouldn't have to leave it to go to the church world. The church needs to equip me to stay where I am at as salt and light." The connecting point for Christian business people and the secular market place is corporate citizenship.

Cary Summers defines corporate citizenship as "effectively serving five shareholders: Equity investors, suppliers, end users (consumers), employees, and the community. The neglect of any one of those five shareholders eventually leads to the deterioration of all five. Therefore, social concern and investment makes good business sense because it builds reputational capital, employee morale, and overall support of the company's marketing and customer relations."

The new era of corporate social concern has even caught on with some of the older and more traditional companies, like IBM.

> [IBM] recently completed its second annual survey of senior executives around the world, asking them how they are handling green and sustainability issues in their corporate strategies. The overwhelming majority of the 224 respondents said they are committed

to incorporating principles of corporate social responsibility into their business strategies—despite the global recession—as a way to improve their business performance, their contribution to society, and their reputation. Some 60% said this was more important to them than a year ago; only 6% said it was less.[3]

IT MAKES GOOD BUSINESS SENSE

"The resulting perception of companies that give back has not changed: In both 1993 and 2008, a full 85 percent of Americans say that they have a more positive image of a product or company when it supports a cause they care about. Today, however, Americans are much more supportive of cause marketing as a way to publicize that support and are more likely to shop with it in mind.

"79 percent would be likely to switch from one brand to another brand, about the same price and quality, if the other brand is associated with a good cause, compared to 66 percent in 1993."[4]

The personal involvement of executives is a great start, but the larger goal is for businesses to involve themselves more fully in compassion endeavors, combining their entrepreneurial knowledge, resources, and employee volunteerism to help make a difference. A number of years ago, Paul Thompson, a former executive for Calloway Golf Foundation, and I convened a group of leading Christian business leaders in Washington DC to discuss ways that the faith community can connect with corporate America and perhaps help facilitate corporate citizenship. Here are some of the helpful ideas that emerged from that conversation.

Cause marketing. Cause marketing is co-branding between a company and a charity to focus on a specific cause or project. It brings needed attention to both the cause and the product the company is offering. For example, the Home Depot Foundation provided $30 million in financial and in-kind support, technical resources, and training to help Habitat for Humanity affiliates build 5000 energy-efficient homes. It was a win-win project for both.

Giving. More and more companies are instituting a payroll deduction campaign so employees can allocate funds to be automatically deducted from their paychecks each month for a company-sponsored social project. The company matches the employee donation to make the money go further, and everyone gets the satisfaction of working together for a worthwhile cause.

Donations. Erick Meier, Convoy of Hope's procurement director, is excited about the potential for maximizing the donations when companies donate some of the products they produce to help meet needs. "Because of our strategic partnerships, we are able to turn every dollar we receive into seven dollars' worth of food and supplies," he says. "We're also able to move product quickly and efficiently throughout the world." For example, "The Coca-Cola North America Company regularly donates drinks such as Powerade and water. Other companies provide cereal, grains, pasta, granola bars, cleaning supplies, canned goods, hygiene kits, school supplies, and more."

Employee volunteerism. Corporate citizenship not only improves the company's image and profits, but according to a study by Boston College, "30 percent of employers say that [it] helps them recruit and retain good employees." America's Incredible Pizza Company, based in Tulsa, has partnered regularly with Convoy of Hope. Rick Barsness, founder and owner, asked all of his employees to consider taking part in Convoy of Hope's "One Day to Feed the World" project. The employees responded enthusiastically and raised thousands of dollars. America's Incredible Pizza Company also donated kitchen equipment that Convoy sent to El Salvador, where it is now being used to help train young people in job skills. Rick says, "This kind of partnership helps us create a healthy environment for our employees as we model our values before them. We are teaching them the importance of giving out of their abundance. I believe every company should provide their employees such opportunities."

WHAT CAN I DO? SOME PRACTICAL WAYS TO MAKE A DIFFERENCE...

- Engage your company in corporate citizenship activities such as volunteerism, giving, or donating goods to a local charity.

- Host a job fair to connect local businesses with those who are unemployed.

- Ask local businesses to donate goods and services to worthy charities in your community.

- Facilitate an annual Business Appreciation Day at your church to honor companies that provide jobs and practice corporate citizenship.

The Army of Corporate Compassion

An emerging trend for companies is to encourage employee participation in community initiatives through employer supported volunteerism (ESV) programs. Such programs allow workers to use some work time to serve at a local charity. According to the Points of Light Foundation, "In 1992 only 31 percent of companies reported using their employee volunteer programs to support core business functions. By 1999, that had increased to 81 percent of all respondents. Moreover, there has been a significant increase in companies that incorporate the volunteer program into the company's overall business plan—an increase from 19 percent in 1992 to 48 percent in 1999."[5] Getting employees involved in volunteer activities sends a message to the community that the business sector is concerned about community issues. Businesses can participate in building up the overall health of the community. Employees in leadership roles in such community outreaches can also raise the visibility of the business while strengthening employee morale and the pride employees have in the company they work for.

Wouldn't it be great to see more businesses at the forefront of the compassion revolution? I have seen the powerful synergy of capitalism and compassion coming together—amazing things happen! God has placed enough expertise and resources on this planet to meet every spiritual, physical, and emotional need. All that's needed is for people to step up and do their part. Business men and women engaged in the compassion revolution will tell you that it's one of the most rewarding parts of their lives.

If you are a business leader and not yet involved in corporate citizenship, perhaps now is the time for you to evaluate how you and your company can get started. The benefits are manifold. Your company increases its visibility and fosters a positive public image, builds a reputation for community involvement, and improves employee loyalty and morale. Your employees learn new skills, enhance their self-worth, and find more meaning and purpose in their vocational life. And the biggest winners of all are the poor because your involvement will strengthen and expand services to lift them from dependency to sustainability.

15

MIRACLES
OF COMPASSION

When we demonstrate the compassion of Jesus to the poor and needy, we bring expressions of His love and His message of hope. We also bring manifestations of His power. Throughout Jesus' ministry, one of the concrete ways He showed His compassion was through His ministry of healing and miracles. More than one-third of the verses in the Gospels are devoted to recording the healing activity of Jesus. For Him, teaching, preaching, and healing were inseparably linked because of His compassionate desire to heal the whole person—spirit, body, and emotions. Many who were blind, deaf, diseased, and disabled received His healing touch.

Jesus commissioned His disciples to carry on that same holistic ministry. As He sent them out, Jesus gave them these instructions: "As you go, preach this message: 'The kingdom of heaven is near.' Heal the sick, raise the dead, cleanse those who have leprosy, drive out demons. Freely you have received, freely give" (Matthew 10:7-8). Physical healings and miracles were part of the manifestation of the coming of His kingdom. Today we preach that same message of the kingdom, the reign of Christ. And through the power of the Holy Spirit this supernatural element of His ministry is still being carried on through His followers. If we are willing, God can use us to bring not only food and hope but also, sometimes, even physical healing.

In our Western world, with so much access to medicine and so many amazing advances in health care, we may not see much need for miraculous healing. After all, we can pay for doctors to give the sick, the lame, and the blind the best possible treatment. But in the developing world, where such medical technologies are not so readily available, sometimes a miracle is the only way someone is likely to be helped.

A Miracle in Calcutta

In 1988 my brothers and I were invited to Calcutta, India, by missionary legend Mark Buntain. Mark has had a powerful ministry there among the poorest of the poor. I had an opportunity to see it in person. But despite everything I had heard about the awful conditions in Calcutta, nothing prepared me for the overwhelming level of need we witnessed.

Traveling from the airport to our hotel, our driver pointed to a large hill in the distance, where a crowd of people were swarming.

"Are those families camping up there?" I naively asked.

"No," he answered, rolling his eyes at my ignorance. "That is the city dump. They are scrounging for food."

At that time, many of Calcutta's 12 million people lived on the streets, seeking food wherever they could find it and existing in unimaginably squalid conditions. As we continued our journey, I saw scores of simple open tents all along the road. It was the only housing available to many poor souls. There, mostly exposed to the elements, many of the old and the diseased died without medical attention. Later in the trip, I watched nuns from Mother Teresa's Sisters of Mercy walk up and down these same roads, checking to see if the people who lived in these ramshackle tents were still alive and, if so, what they might need. To my horror, every day many died from lack of food or untreated disease. The scope of the problem felt overwhelming.

Mark asked my brothers and me to speak at some of the churches he had planted among the very poor on the outskirts of Calcutta. It was a privilege to bring the gospel to these poor, whom Jesus loved so much. When I preached, though, I drew stares of wonderment because of my white skin. "They have heard of white men before," the pastor confided to me, "but you are the first they have seen."

It was kind of a blow to my ego. I thought they had come to hear my preaching, but many were actually just interested in gawking at the strange pale man! I was the town freak show!

At the close of one of the services, I invited people who needed physical healing to come forward for prayer. A middle-aged woman stepped forward. Only later did I learn she was the daughter of the village chief. My eye was immediately drawn to her right foot, because it was deformed and turned almost 180 degrees.

Before I could even lay hands on her and declare all the words of faith I had learned in seminary, something started to happen to the woman's foot. As she walked around the front of the church, her foot began to straighten out before all our watching eyes. Her steps became hops. Her arms flailed about. Bystanders ducked for cover. Uncontrolled emotion overtook the entire room as people witnessed a miracle—the woman had been healed!

"Hope you plan on staying for the rest of the night," the pastor said with an amazed smile, "because you're not leaving until the whole village is prayed for!" And indeed, the word spread quickly throughout the village that the chief's daughter had been healed. Within minutes a line stretched from the altar area where the pastor and I were standing, as far as I could see.

The villagers had heard the message of God's love and compassion before, but now they were witnessing it in genuine fashion. Through the healing, the preaching of Jesus' good news earned a new respect among the villagers.

Signs and Wonders

When John the Baptist was languishing in prison and beginning to doubt whether Jesus was the real thing after all, he sent some of his followers to ask the Lord if He really was the expected Messiah. How did Jesus respond to this question? He pointed to both the message and the miracles: "The blind receive sight, the lame walk, those who have leprosy are cured, the deaf hear, the dead are raised, and the good news is preached to the poor" (Matthew 11:5). In essence, Jesus was saying, "Tell John that I have the credentials. My actions authenticate me as the Messiah." Those actions included a combination of preaching the good news to the poor and performing miracles.

The writer of Hebrews emphasizes the role that signs and wonders play in the reception of the gospel: "How shall we escape if we ignore such a great salvation? This salvation, which was first announced by the Lord, was confirmed to us by those who heard him. God also testified to it by signs, wonders and various miracles, and gifts of the Holy Spirit distributed according to his will" (Hebrews 2:3-4). Christians in the early centuries of the church were not afraid to combine the message of the good news with a demonstration of its power. We learn from Acts 5:14-16 that the apostle Peter took advantage of miraculous healings as a way to invite people into a relationship with God. This is certainly one of the reasons why the message of Jesus spread so quickly throughout Asia Minor.

Healing for Social Outcasts

Sometimes physical healing and "social healing" go hand in hand. The Gospels record a number of occasions when Jesus healed sufferers of leprosy, a highly infectious disease that disfigures and wastes away the flesh. This disease is so contagious, in fact, that its victims were quarantined in remote places in order to separate them from others who might get infected (Leviticus 13:45-46). You might say they were victims twice over—physically impaired and socially isolated.

But while others avoided the lepers at all costs, Jesus reached out to them—literally. He not only allowed them to approach Him but also touched them, laying hands on them in order to heal them (Mark 1:40-42). Jesus broke through the societal conventions that kept them at arm's length, putting Himself at risk in order to bring healing—and the healing power of acceptance—to those who were social outcasts.

How close do we allow the "unclean" and the "outcasts" of our day to get to us before we back away? Leprosy may not be very common today, but many of the poor suffer from other problems that cause us to avoid them, either out of fear or embarrassment. I remember the way many Christians recoiled against those suffering from HIV/AIDS when the epidemic first manifested itself. It's difficult not to avert our eyes in fear of the many homeless who suffer from mental disorders.

How will those in need experience the loving, unconditional embrace of our Savior if we are too embarrassed or afraid to be with them, too intimidated to sit next to them, or too busy to get to know them well enough to pray for them?

Compassionate Praying

Miracles begin with prayer, so prayer is a fundamental activity for every compassion revolutionary. It taps into the source of the power that brings healing to the needy and desperate. When our own resources and expertise are not enough, sometimes people need God's direct healing touch to come to them. And we are the hands and feet of Jesus as He brings that miraculous touch. But it all begins with prayer.

Our days are filled with dozens of urgencies and emergencies, all vying for our attention. Sometimes these are the emergencies of the people we are trying to help. Stopping to pray can seem counterproductive when we feel as if we should be *doing* something! At times our focus on doing good works of compassion can be so all-consuming that we forget to pray. But the miracles, both big and small, that God performs when we pray are an indispensible part of reaching out. People need not only food, water, shelter, and medicine but also a healing touch from God.

God uses prayer to equip us for compassion miracles in a number of ways.

Prayer releases the Holy Spirit to work through us. Some believe that "if you do your best, God will do the rest," as if we are in a 50/50 partnership. But our human resources are so very limited that we are much more likely to succeed when we trust in His power. Miracles happen when we become yielded instruments of God to accomplish His will!

The disciples were apprentices, learning how to minister as Jesus ministered. When they were sent out to preach and to heal, they sometimes found themselves unable to effect the miracles they sought. When they asked Jesus why, He pointed to their limited faith and gave them this promise: "I tell you the truth, if you have faith as small as a mustard seed, you can say to this mountain, 'Move from here to there' and it will move. Nothing will be impossible for you" (Matthew 17:20). That is quite a promise. We may not be in the practice of regularly moving mountains, but when we are involved in compassion ministries, we are sure to come up against mountain-sized problems again and again. This is exactly the time we need to learn to pray and to lean on the Holy Spirit to work through us.

The apostle Paul assures us, "The Spirit helps us in our weakness. We do not know what we ought to pray for, but the Spirit himself intercedes for us with groans that words cannot express. And he who searches our hearts knows the mind of the Spirit, because the Spirit intercedes for the saints in accordance with God's will" (Romans 8:26-27). Paul is reminding the Christians in Rome—and us—that the Holy Spirit is praying *through* us to accomplish the will of the Father.

Prayer makes us sensitive to the needs of others. When we make prayer a priority in our lives, we begin to pay attention. Prayer opens our eyes so we can see more clearly and more compassionately. Everything that is happening around us becomes a topic for conversation with God as we bring to Him all the needs of which we become aware.

If we are in communion with God through prayer, our lives can become adventures of divine appointments. In these adventures, our days are filled with people and events that God brings our way so that we might partner with Him in meeting needs. This is an amazing and exciting way to live!

One morning I had a very strong impression from the Lord that my path was going to intersect with a man running from his family. This was one of those times when I was confident that God was speaking to my heart. Sure enough, later that morning I was cruising down the freeway when I spotted a gentleman walking away from his car with a gas can in hand. Knowing the closest service station was miles away, I stopped to give him a lift.

We chatted on the way to the service station, and I learned that his name was Tom and that he was going through a difficult time in his life. I felt the nudge of the Spirit that this was the divine appointment for which He had been preparing me. "Tom, during my prayer time this morning God revealed to me that I would meet you today and that you would be running from Him and from your family."

He looked at me wide-eyed, knowing that a stranger like me could not possibly be acquainted with his story. He started weeping. Between the sobs, he revealed that he had drifted away from God and that his life had spiraled out of control. That very moment he had decided to leave his family, but in his haste he didn't check the gas tank. He ended up alongside the road with an empty tank and a heart full of pain. That's when God miraculously reached out to him, and I happened to be the instrument He used.

"God loves you so much that He sent me to look for you," I told him. "Are you ready to return to Him and to your family?"

"Yes," he said, "I'm ready."

After we refilled his car, he invited me back to his home, where I prayed with him, his wife, and his children, asking God to give them a new start—a fresh beginning. As I left, he was hugging his wife and children. The prodigal dad had come home.

My part in the story was simply to believe in God's compassion, to be available to be used, and to put my prayers into practice. Just as the disciples were sent out in the book of Acts to all corners of the globe to share God's love "with signs following" (Mark 16:20 kjv), so we will see God at work if we are willing to be partners with Him.

Prayer can accomplish more than we can imagine. Prayer transcends our human limitations. When faced with friends or family members who are dispirited or depressed, acquaintances who have lost jobs or seen their marriages collapse, or strangers seemingly captive to mental dysfunction, we often simply don't know what to do or say to help them. Our hearts ache for them, but all our words seem hollow and our solutions inadequate. But the God who is beyond time and space is big enough to touch anyone in even the direst or most complicated situation. No problem is too big for God.

George Mueller ran an orphanage that saved the lives of many thousands of orphans. He made a policy of never turning away any child who needed help, which meant that finances and resources were always a challenge. But Mueller was a man of deep faith and fervent prayer. Whenever he saw a need, he prayed. To remind himself of God's provision, he kept a journal of all the answers to his prayers. When he added them up late in his life, he could list more than 50,000 specifically answered prayers! He noted that about 5000 of them were answered on the very day that he prayed. This was his formula for ministry: "The Lord pours in while we seek to pour out."

The Faith of Children

Mueller ran an orphanage in England, but I experienced a miracle of provision during a trip to El Salvador. In this particular instance, the other visitors and I were the answer to the prayers!

I was on a bus filled with pastors and business leaders from America who were on a fact-finding trip through this small Central American nation. We were looking for ways to help the poor in this part of the world. After a long journey we pulled up in front of an old orphanage, where the children suddenly came rushing out of the dorms and running toward us. They were laughing, smiling, and jumping up and down. "Now *that*," said one of the pastors, "is a greeting!"

The director of the orphanage approached us with nearly equal joy and excitement. "We have been praying for you!" he said.

"Praying for us?" I asked.

"Yes, we ran out of food yesterday, so the children have been praying for God to feed us."

Moments later, one of our Convoy of Hope vehicles arrived with rice, beans, and—oh yes, pizzas—for everyone. Before our arrival, none of us were aware of the desperate needs. But God knew, and He had used us to answer the prayers of these little ones. The God who oversees the whole world can orchestrate events and answer people's prayers through you and me.

Prayer can transform the atmosphere. As we partner with God in prayer, He can powerfully change the whole tenor of a place, a neighborhood…even a nation. Many times police officers on duty at our community outreaches are shocked to see peace and love and cooperation in areas that are usually marked by anger, violence, and despair. They see their beats transformed, at least for a few hours, into places of hope.

If you have ever been on a prayer walk, you know how powerful this can be. In a prayer walk, members of a community representing all ages and backgrounds convene at a local church for a time of praise and worship. Then they take it to the streets! They walk slowly through the troubled areas of the community, singing and praying for God to deliver their community from violence, addictions, prostitution, and hopelessness. Many have testified about the "wake of peace" that follows these marches. The presence of God's praying people makes a difference.

Light Breaks Forth!

Isaiah prophesied that when you give yourself to the poor, "your light will break forth like the dawn, and your healing will quickly appear; then your righteousness will go before you, and the glory of the LORD will be your rear guard" (Isaiah 58:8).

A scientist placed a plant in a room with closed curtains and no light. He was experimenting to see how long it would take for the plant to die from lack of sunlight. As the days passed, the petals wilted and turned brown. What had once been a beautiful plant with stunning colors and a lovely scent was now struggling to survive.

Preparing to leave on a trip, the scientist checked his experiment one last time before he walked out the door. In his haste, he accidently brushed against the curtain, and it was left slightly open, allowing a sliver of light to enter the dark room. He was in too much of a hurry to even notice.

When he returned, he expected to find the plant completely dead. But something mysterious had happened. The plant was not dead, but very much alive. The scientist discovered that the branches of the plant were stretching out toward the thin beam of light that came through the slightly parted curtains. That little bit of light sustained the plant, even in nearly complete darkness.

I think that is a beautiful picture of compassion miracles. Through prayer, we let God's light into a dark place. We need acts of kindness and caring. Absolutely. But we should also be praying and believing that God is partnering with us in the work we are doing. And His power is so far beyond ours.

Some Christians think that miracles are a thing of the past—only for the biblical times. Perhaps they are afraid of the craziness and excesses and deception that some have practiced in the name of the supernatural. How sad if the phonies and hypocrites scare us away from experiencing one of the powerful ways that we can demonstrate compassion—miracles. Shane Claiborne tells an amazing story about how God can take the little we have to offer and turn it into a miracle.

> A friend of mine was working down in Latin America in a health clinic they had set up. They had very few supplies, and one day they had run out of everything except a bottle of Pepto-Bismol. So when people showed up with all sorts of illnesses, all they could offer them was Pepto. But then, my friend says, "The crazy thing is people were getting healed." They were coming with all sorts of illnesses and injuries, and the missionaries would give them Pepto. A crowd of folks gathered from all over, and he said that somehow that little bottle never ran out.[1]

Christians from the developed nations can easily dismiss the reality of God's ongoing supernatural intervention in the lives of His people. We can turn to our medicine and counseling and modern technologies and techniques. In the developing world, though, it is a very different story. As one African leader said to me, "We do not just believe in miracles. We depend on them."

WHAT CAN I DO? SOME PRACTICAL WAYS TO MAKE A DIFFERENCE...

- Pray daily that God will build your faith in His ability to work miracles.
- Look for opportunities to pray for people who have physical, emotional, and financial needs.
- Develop a prayer group at your church, business, or school.

Silver and Gold

> One day Peter and John were going up to the temple at the time of prayer—at three in the afternoon. Now a man crippled from birth was being carried to the temple gate called Beautiful, where he was put every day to beg from those going into the temple courts. When he saw Peter and John about to enter, he asked them for money. Peter looked straight at him, as did John. Then Peter said, "Look at us!" So the man gave them his attention, expecting to get something from them.

> Then Peter said, "Silver or gold I do not have, but what I have I give you. In the name of Jesus Christ of Nazareth, walk." Taking him by the right hand, he helped him up, and instantly the man's feet and ankles became strong. He jumped to his feet and began to walk. Then he went with them into the temple courts, walking and jumping, and praising God. When all the people saw him walking and praising God, they recognized him as the same man who used to sit begging at the temple gate called Beautiful, and they were filled with wonder and amazement at what had happened to him (Acts 3:1-9).

As compassion revolutionaries, let's be open to being used by God to offer hope, compassion, and healing for the whole person. Sometimes that may mean having the courage to act in faith, believing that God can accomplish what no human ingenuity can manage. Perhaps miracles of compassion can begin to happen when we start declaring, "Silver and gold *I have*, but I want to give you something even better. In the name of Jesus Christ of Nazareth, walk!"

REVOLUTIONARY GIVING

At a Convoy of Hope outreach in Winston-Salem, North Carolina, our volunteers got a chance to practice the kind of generosity that is the surest sign of true compassion revolutionaries. In a small but very real way, they were able to show what it means to care enough to sacrifice some of their own comfort so that others might find a little comfort themselves.

It was a blisteringly cold fall day, the kind of day where the cold is insistent and inescapable. Our volunteers had come prepared. They left their homes dressed in warm jackets, stocking caps, gloves, and wool socks, ready to deal with the harsh conditions. But many of our guests from the community, who had lined up at the gate to wait for the event to open, were visibly shivering. Many of them didn't own any warm clothes.

One of the volunteers from a local church saw the disparity and decided to do something about it. Without any fanfare, he removed his coat and wrapped it around a shivering child. Others followed suit, taking off their hats, coats, and scarves and giving them to those who didn't have anything to protect them from the cold.

Now it was the volunteers' turn to shiver for a while, but inside I know they were warmed by the sense of joy that comes from being able to help others by giving. The smile on the faces of volunteers and guests was priceless, and more than a few eyes were left a little moist!

Where Your Heart Is

In this chapter I am going to talk a lot about money. But I wanted to start with that story because it demonstrates the heart that lies beneath financial generosity. It points out that giving is not just a religious duty, but a joyous way to make a difference in the lives of others. Revolutionary giving can be both satisfying and exciting—and life-changing!

The old saying goes that "some things are better caught than taught." Jesus showed His own generosity time and again throughout His ministry, offering His time and His resources to help the needy multitudes that heard about Him and came for help, healing, and hope. He clearly held on to possessions lightly, and He instructed His disciples to do the same: "Sell your possessions and give to the poor. Provide purses for yourselves that will not wear out, a treasure in heaven that will not be exhausted, where no thief comes near and no moth destroys. For where your treasure is, there your heart will be also" (Luke 12:33-34). Jesus reminded them of how temporary and transient objects and cash really are, and He challenged them to put their money where their heart was—in an investment that would reap eternal rewards.

Our hearts are often tied to our pocketbooks, so Jesus talked a lot about money and how we are to handle it. You might be surprised to learn that about 15 percent of Jesus' words recorded in the Gospels deal with this issue. Another old adage claims that polite people don't talk about religion or money, but these are two of the things that Jesus spoke the most about. And He saw a deep connection between them. The way we use our money shows a lot about what we really believe and reveals our true priorities. The apostle John echoed this very sentiment. "If anyone has material possessions and sees his brother in need but has no pity on him, how can the love of God be in him? Dear children, let us not love with words or tongue, but with actions and in truth" (1 John 3:17-18).

The book of Acts gives us a clear picture of how literally the early followers of Jesus practiced this priority. "All the believers were together and had everything in common. Selling their possessions and goods, they gave to anyone as he had need" (Acts 2:44-45).

Your Deserted Island

Sometimes you can have an epiphany while watching a movie.

It happened for me while viewing the Tom Hanks film *Cast Away*. In the film, Hanks plays Chuck, a FedEx employee whose cargo plane crashes near a deserted island in the South Pacific. Chuck soon realizes that he has been given up as lost and must find a way to fend for himself in this sometimes hostile environment. He is hungry and lonely but not willing to give up. He receives a wonderful boon when several of the FedEx packages he was carrying in the plane wash up on shore. These packages contain various items that he is able to use to survive, and he eventually concocts a way to escape from the island.

As I watched the film, the thought occurred to me, *If I were marooned on a deserted island with other castaways and blessed with the resources to survive, would I share them with others on the island?* I think all of us, whether followers of Jesus or not, know that would be the only right thing to do. But what happens on this global island called Earth? There are 6.7 billion people on our planet, and nearly four billion of them live on less than two dollars a day. In his book *Rich Christians in an Age of Hunger*, Ron Sider reminds us of our real situation. "The poorest 20% of the people (just over one billion) own 1% of the world's wealth...The richest 20% own 81%."[1]

There is a widening gap between the haves and the have-nots.

The apostle Paul spoke about this disparity between the haves and the have-nots and the need for more equality: "Our desire is not that others might be relieved while you are hard pressed, but that there might be equality. At the present time your plenty will supply what they need, so that in turn their plenty will supply what you need. Then there will be equality" (2 Corinthians 8:13-14).

And what is God's plan for equality? Sider contends that the biblical understanding of economic equality demands at least this: "God wants every person and family to have equality of opportunity, at least to the point of having access to the resources necessary (land, money, education), so that by working responsibly they can earn a decent living and participate as dignified members of their community."[2] Doesn't that strike you as right? That all God's children deserve a chance—an opportunity to have their basic needs met and to be able to improve their conditions by responsible labor? That is why giving is so important. Our sharing provides others the chance to survive and thrive. Our money is the most common tool God uses to make this a reality.

God's Plan for Giving

Let's examine a couple of the strategies God has instituted for giving and for meeting the needs of the community.

The tithe is a primary biblical method of giving. Our word *tithe* comes from an Old English root word meaning "one-tenth." That is exactly what the Old Testament refers to as the tithe. In Old Testament times, Israel's economy was based on agriculture, so the call for a tithe was primarily applied to crops and livestock (Leviticus 27:30-32; Deuteronomy 14:22,26; 26:1-2). Its primary purpose was to support the Levites, who served as the priests, and for upkeep of the temple (Numbers 18:21). The tithe is also referred to as the firstfruits of one's harvest, as in Proverbs 3:9-10, where blessing is promised to those who give one-tenth of their yield: "Honor the LORD with your wealth, with the firstfruits of all your crops; then your barns will be filled to overflowing, and your vats will brim with new wine." In fact, the Israelites commonly gathered the harvest into piles and then allowed the Levitical priests to collect the top 10 percent of the piles as the firstfruits.

Not surprisingly, some neglected this practice, wanting to keep it all for themselves. But when they disobeyed in this manner, God's prophets underscored both the judgment that would come from disobedience and the blessing that would come from obedience:

"You are under a curse—the whole nation of you—because you are robbing me. Bring the whole tithe into the storehouse, that there may be food in my house. Test me in this," says the LORD of hosts, "and see if I will not throw open the floodgates of heaven and pour out so much blessing that you will not have room enough for it. I will prevent pests from devouring your crops, and the vines in your field will not cast their fruit" (Malachi 3:9-11).

This Old Testament pattern of giving 10 percent has become a model that many Christians have chosen to follow in their own giving.

Another method of giving in biblical times was to leave the corners of the fields unharvested in order to provide for needy people. As we saw earlier, God instructed the Israelites, "When you reap the harvest of your land, you shall not wholly reap the corners of your field when you reap, nor shall you gather any gleaning from your harvest. You shall leave them for the poor and for the stranger. I am the LORD your God" (Leviticus 23:22 NKJV).

It All Belongs to Him

The basis of understanding God's perspective on giving is to acknowledge that it all belongs to Him. You belong to God, and everything you own belongs to God. King David understood this: "Wealth and honor come from you" (1 Chronicles 29:12). If everything we have belongs to God, and if, as we have clearly seen, helping the poor is a God-given priority for you and me, then doesn't it make sense that a portion of our time and money should go to those in need?

Our culture promotes this attitude: *I've worked hard for my money, and I deserve to be comfortable.* We are taught that self-interest is good for the economy. And though it does in some ways help the economy grow, it cannot be the bottom line for God's people. We need to swim against the tide of consumerism and consumption and be willing to give our money to further God's purposes and God's priorities. Second Corinthians 9:11 reminds us that God has blessed us so that we can bless others: "You will be made rich in every way so that you can be generous on every occasion."

WHAT CAN I DO? SOME PRACTICAL WAYS TO MAKE A DIFFERENCE...

- Study what the Bible has to say about giving and the promises of God's blessings (see appendix 1).

- Determine how much money you need to live on and how much you desire to give away to your church and other worthy organizations.

- Become an advocate for a charity by challenging others to give generously.

Have You Been Supersized?

My intent is not to make you feel guilty. I have found no place in the Bible where guilt is used as a motivating factor in helping the poor. God wants us to focus on pleasing Him by meeting the needs of our fellow human beings, not to respond in order to relieve guilty feelings. We each need to take an honest, personal, internal audit to see how and why we spend our money. Then we can compare what we learn with what God knows is best for our world and for us.

Morgan Spurlock undertook an experiment and even made a movie about it. In his documentary *Super Size Me,* Spurlock decided to explore what would happen if he ate nothing but food from MacDonald's for 30 days. In only 5 days he gained almost ten pounds. By the time the 30 days were over, he had gained so much weight that he took 14 months to return to his original weight. His experiment also had predictably bad effects on his mental and physical well-being. He had nearly supersized himself into serious liver dysfunction and severe depression.

This film is an accurate commentary on the way we tend to live our lives in the modern Western world. According to the Self-Storage Association, we Americans now possess more than two billion square feet of storage space outside our own homes. As large as most people's homes are these days, they still don't have room for all their stuff. Many families can no longer use their garages for their cars because they need the room for all their junk. And when even the garage isn't enough, they rent storage space so they have a place to stash it all! The past decade has seen a 75 percent increase in rented storage space even though the average size of a home has expanded by nearly 1000 square feet and families have grown smaller.

Think about it. Even though we have bigger homes and smaller families, we still need an additional two billion square feet of rented space to store our stuff. Believe me, I am not immune. I purchased a book called *How to Clean Out the Clutter,* but now I can't find it because it got lost in all my clutter!

We have been brainwashed into thinking that larger homes, luxury cars, and expensive gadgets are the path to a meaningful existence—a vicious cycle of "It's more blessed to receive than to give." Is its grip on us so strong that we can't even distinguish anymore between necessities and luxuries?

In a world of supersizing, we need to develop a "theology of enough." John Wesley practiced this by determining how much he needed to live on—to meet his essentials—and then giving all the rest away. Can you imagine the impact if numbers of Christians adopted this value system?

Is it too radical to ask ourselves how much is enough when most of the world doesn't have enough to survive? Can we embrace a revolutionary lifestyle that redefines the idea of the good life? Perhaps we need to meditate on the wisdom of Proverbs 23:4: "Do not wear yourselves out to get rich; have the wisdom to show restraint." Remember that these words come from Solomon, one of the richest men who ever lived, and one who had learned by experience that the priorities of wealth could derail a person from God's priorities. Toward the end of his life he concluded, "I have seen all the things that are done under the sun; all of them are meaningless, a chasing after the wind" (Ecclesiastes 1:14). The things we give away, not the things we keep, will define our happiness.

17

RESPONSIBLE
COMPASSION

When I was still a young man, I learned an important lesson about the connection between compassion and responsibility. Once my mother, my siblings, and I got reestablished in a home of our own, Pastor Horwege occasionally dropped by to check on Mom and see how we were all doing. On one visit he huddled with us kids in the front yard, gathering us together like a quarterback getting ready to call a play.

Our front yard was nothing more than a patch of dirt, which became a muddy swamp when the rains came. So we were all very excited when he announced that the church board had voted to bless us with a front lawn. We all jumped up and down with unrestrained glee over the prospect of having real grass to play on.

But our euphoria was dampened a bit by what he said next. "There's one catch. You won't receive the entire lawn at once. We'll start with one strip of grass. If you care for that one piece and keep it green, then we'll keep adding strips until you have a full lawn."

It sounded like a practical joke, but he wasn't kidding. Days later the first strip of sod was laid in our front yard near the house. The neighbors gawked with curiosity. One even asked, "Who's buried under there?"

At first the grass received much attention and appeared to respond favorably to our tender loving care. Yet over time, other priorities—golfing, camping, and, oh yes, school—began to crowd out the development of our green thumbs.

The plush green grass faded into a brownish-yellow layer of crusty dirt.

Pastor kept his word and never brought us another strip of grass. And we learned a valuable lesson: If someone is gracious enough to give us something, we are responsible to be good stewards of that gift.

Personal Responsibility

Genuine compassion requires responsibility both in giving and receiving. As we have seen, God has a special place in His heart for the poor and a special blessing for those who show compassion toward them. But sometimes compassion, if not offered wisely, is actually counterproductive to the long-term good of its recipient. Irresponsible compassion can have a negative effect on how the poor estimate their personal value and their place in society.

The Bible says, "Carry each other's burdens" (Galatians 6:2). But it also admonishes that "each one should carry his own load" (Galatians 6:5). The goal of helping people is that they might—if they are able—learn to help themselves. Responsible compassion is not about giving endless handouts. It is about giving people a "hand up" so they may, in turn, be able to help others.

For example, we've seen that the practice of gleaning was one of the key ways that the needs of the poor, the widows, and the orphans were to be met. The owners of the land were to leave the excess of the harvest, but the hungry had to take the initiative to meet their own needs. God could have simply commanded that a portion of the harvest be given to the poor, but instead He provided the needy with a way to work toward meeting their own needs and to experience the dignity that comes with labor.

In our culture, we tend to think of labor as a necessary evil, and we constantly look for ways to reduce the human effort of producing and distributing goods. We are excited about the newest labor-saving devices, as though labor were something to be avoided whenever possible. We believe that the purpose of our lives is found in leisure rather than work, and that our work is just what we have to do so we can have fun later.

But this is not God's perspective. Even in the idyllic Garden of Eden, the earthly paradise, there was work to be done. Plants produce fruit, vegetables must be harvested, crops must be cared for, and animals need to be domesticated. There is a natural goodness in labor that adds self-respect and meaning to human lives. We were never meant to spend all our time in lazy pleasures.

So when we help the poor, we help them best by letting them participate in that help whenever possible. Responsible compassion requires that both the giver and receiver of charity participate in God's plan for meeting basic human needs.

Beyond Win-Win

My brother Steve created a model for helping the poor through a thrift store called New Tags. New Tags receives clothing donated from local churches and then sells it to the economically challenged at very low prices. Whenever I visit this store, I love to see the satisfaction of customers paying for their goods with their own money and with the knowledge they are getting a great deal! This is what I call "beyond win-win" compassion.

First, the churches are blessed by following Jesus' command to clothe the naked; second, New Tags sells the clothing and uses its profits to fund a nonprofit organization called Rural Compassion (which helps the needy in rural areas with outreaches and disaster relief); and third, the poor are given the opportunity to buy good clothing at amazing prices—with the satisfaction of shopping for and choosing what they purchase with their own funds. Plus, it allows them to stretch their limited funds so they can use them in meeting other needs, such as food, electricity, and transportation. Everybody wins—and then some!

In our compassion outreach, we want to avoid creating a sense of dependency. As Robert Lupton, who has been serving the poor in Atlanta for more than 35 years, agonizes, "When we see the same families show up week after week at our church food pantry, we can't help questioning (though very privately) whether we are helping them get on their feet or whether we are fostering their dependency."[1] When the poor begin to depend on a handout rather than receiving a hand up, we are failing them.

Of course, some abuse the system. Charity abuse can become like substance abuse, as recipients rely on crutches that are ultimately destructive to their self-worth and dignity. This misuse provides a poor role model for their children. The abuse of charity has led to increased scrutiny and new methods of accountability. I applaud these steps. I am saddened to think that in some cases we are creating "charity junkies" who eventually lose the impetus and desire to help themselves. That is why systems of responsibility and accountability are so very important.

A Hand Up, Not a Handout

Amy Sherman describes one such accountability system.

> Individuals with emergency financial needs must meet face-to-face
> with a church counselor. During the interview they must explain
> their situation and show relevant documentation—such as an evic-
> tion notice from the landlord or a "cut-off" notice from the electrical
> power company. They must also disclose information about their
> sources of income—pay stubs from their jobs or documentation
> describing their public assistance benefits.[2]

The church counselor verifies the information and then writes the check
directly to the landlord or power company.

If these procedures seem harsh or uncompassionate to you, think about
how much money and resources that could go to the truly needy are being
wasted on the merely lazy and indigent. By weeding out the charity abusers, we can expand services to those who need them most. This is simply a
matter of good stewardship.

In his letter to Timothy, Paul instructs the young church leader to practice
responsible compassion to the widows, a category of the needy that receives
much attention in the Bible. Paul suggested requirements for widows who
were to receive help: "No widow may be put on the list of widows unless
she is over sixty, has been faithful to her husband, and is well-known for her
good deeds, such as bringing up children, showing hospitality, washing the
feet of the saints, helping those in trouble and devoting herself to all kinds of
good deeds" (1 Timothy 5:9-10). Paul wanted to reward the faithful, caring,
hardworking widows, not those who were idle or self-centered.

Some churches have focused on creating jobs for homeless men and
women as the best way of helping them out. Workers start at a low wage,
but if they demonstrate a good work ethic—punctuality, dependability, and
a positive attitude—they can receive a wage increase. The goal is to provide
workers with opportunities to build self-esteem and good résumés by demonstrating that they can dig themselves out of their financial distress. As
Ron Sider points out, "Most of the poor do not want a handout but desire
to earn their own way. They have enormous social capital: intact families, a
desire to work, pride, integrity. But they need some help."[3]

Millions of people need and deserve a safety net. Perhaps they are unable
to work due to physical or mental illness. Maybe they lost their job and

haven't been able to find a new one, or they just need a short-term backup due to a crisis in their life. The welfare system was created to meet such needs for temporary assistance through government programs, but the system was never meant to create a group of people who have lost the will to help themselves and who would rather live on the public dole even though they are perfectly capable of working.

Responsible compassion includes teaching skills.

Changing a Culture of Dependency

Noted author and commentator Marvin Olasky has chronicled the increase in government assistance among the American populace. When the major economic crisis emerged in the early 1930s, he says, many turned to the government to meet their needs. Meanwhile, many private charities and churches surrendered their work. The result, he claims, has been decades where the government has essentially had a monopoly on caring. He shared these thoughts in a conversation with me:

> Over the past three decades, we have fought a war on poverty that has also struck down three of the best allies against poverty: shame,

family, and God. When we take away shame, we take away deterrence. When we take away family, we take away the soil in which compassion best grows. When we kick out religion, we also remove the greatest incentive to help and be helped.

During the 1950s, Aid for Dependent Children (AFDC) rolls rose by 17 percent, but during the 1960s, the increase was 107 percent. Above three-fourths of that increase occurred from 1965 to 1968 alone during a time of general prosperity and diminishing unemployment.

Olasky says that most Americans like the way a welfare system, corrupt and inefficient though it is, removes the burden of basic care from our consciences. "Church leaders forgot that compassion means *suffering with*; they looked more and more to government to fulfill the biblical mandate to 'care for the least of these.'" Olasky advocates seven principles for practicing responsible compassion that can restore the church's moral authority and effectively reengage believers with the plight of the poor.

1. *Affiliation (connect with families and community).* Responsible compassion begins with first trying to restore family ties.

2. *Bonding (help one by one).* Effective compassion is often a personalized, face-to-face approach.

3. *Categorization (treat different problems differently).* For example, those who are orphaned, elderly, or disabled receive aid. Jobless adults who are able and willing to work receive help finding a job. (This is something Convoy of Hope endeavors to do at its citywide outreaches.)

4. *Discernment (give responsibly).* We must help wisely—giving with our heads as well as our hearts.

5. *Employment (give priority).* Programs that stress employment, sometimes in creative new ways, need greater emphasis and deserve our support.

6. *Freedom (reduce barriers to compassion and enterprise).* Be intentional in networking charities to enterprise.

7. *God (reliance on the Creator and His providence).* Successful

antipoverty work, past and present, has allowed the poor to earn authentic self-esteem not by offering easy, feel-good praise, but by pointing them to God.

It Needs Fixing

During a Convoy of Hope outreach in New Orleans, we decided to take groceries to families living in the housing projects. The narrow halls of these complexes were damp, cold, dark, and depressing. Cries of children echoed from within the walls. As we knocked on one of the apartment doors, a woman yelled from inside, "Who is it?"

"We are from Convoy of Hope, and we wanted to give you some groceries," I said through the door. Evidently that was the right password because the door swung open. Before me stood a young woman with a baby in her arms. She was obviously still in her teens but already had a baby and two toddlers who were peering at us from behind their mother's legs. She asked us to place the groceries on the table.

"Is there anything we can pray with you about?" I asked.

"Yes," she answered. "My boyfriend just left me, and I don't know how I can raise these kids on my own."

"Do you have any family that can help?"

"I'd rather live with my mom and have her care for the kids so I can go to school, but I have to be on my own to receive the government money."

The brokenness of this woman's situation and her value system are deeply troubling. She is not married but has three children to raise all by herself. Her only source of financial support comes from a government program (Aid for Dependent Children—AFDC) that will increase her income only if she bears more children and lives on her own.

If you think this is a rare circumstance, think again. Children raising children on the public dole is a way of life for millions. Fifty percent of unmarried women of all ages go on AFDC soon after their first child. Think about the irony of a well-meaning government system that actually creates incentives for bearing babies out of wedlock and marginalizes single moms from their families.

Before we cast stones from our glass houses, however, let's remember that these government systems became necessary because the church abdicated its moral and biblical mandate to care for the needy. This meant that the government had to provide a social safety net. If Christians were doing their jobs in accordance with what Scripture teaches, the government programs wouldn't be so essential. Perhaps the best way of thinking about the government welfare system is that for all its faults, it is like Noah's ark—it stinks, but it's still the best thing afloat.

At the end of the day, irresponsible compassion—whether it is practiced by the government or the church—will breed a welfare mentality that erodes away the self-worth of the people who are supposedly being helped. Their incentive slackens, their dreams die, and survival becomes the only goal in life. As Robert Lupton reminds us, "When society subsidizes you for being noncontributory, it has added insult to your already injured self-esteem."[5]

S.H.A.P.E. Up!

So what can be done to change this self-destructive mind-set and these systems that keep people trapped in their poverty? I like to say, if you do the right things, right things will happen. We may not be able to change the system all by ourselves, but we can start making personal choices that reflect responsible compassion. Here are four keys to making a difference:

First, determine what you have to offer. God has empowered you with assets that you can use to make a difference. I like to use the acronym S.H.A.P.E. to help people determine what they might have to give:

- *Spiritual gifts.* You'll find a helpful spiritual gift test at www.elmertowns.com.

- *Heart's desire.* What is your passion for service?

- *Abilities.* What God-given talents do you possess that you can use to serve others?

- *Participation.* Can you volunteer to serve the poor through your church or a local community organization?

- *Evaluation.* After several months of service, ask a pastor or lay leader to assess your service and evaluate whether this area of ministry is compatible with your gifts, desires, and abilities.

Second, decide to use your talents. Some people would say, "These are good principles to follow, but I'll need more time and money if I'm going to do something about them." Some may defer getting involved to a later date, when they will supposedly be in a better position in life to help. But you shouldn't wait for the perfect opportunity. It will likely never come. My good friend Tommy Barnett likes to say, "Find a need and fill it!" Responsible compassion is using whatever you have *right now* to make a difference.

Third, research nonprofit organizations. Before you give, take the time to learn a little about the needs, who is meeting them, and the organization's goals and philosophies. Some are much more effective and get more bang for their buck than others. Some are based on more biblically solid principles than others. Learn about where your money is going. Don't just send off some money to the most well-known organizations in order to provide immediate relief for your conscience. Make sure to put your money to work where it will work the best.

Appendix 4, "Some Recommended Compassion Organizations," lists some Christian organizations that I believe are worthy of financial support and volunteer service. This of course is in addition to the giving and serving you should be doing at your home church. A good resource worth checking out is Charity Navigator at www.charitynavigator.org, the largest independent charity evaluator.

Fourth, volunteer to serve. Get personally involved instead of just paying someone else to do it. You will discover so much joy and meaning in actually getting your hands dirty on behalf of the poor. It is an adventure that will help you grow in compassion, understanding, and grace as you get to know the needy as people, not just statistics!

WHAT CAN I DO? SOME PRACTICAL WAYS TO MAKE A DIFFERENCE...

- Use the S.H.A.P.E method to evaluate your participation in local, national, and international organizations that are worthy of your time and financial support.

- After several months of giving and/or volunteering, meet with the leadership of the charity to evaluate the results of your investment.

- Help promote charities you have evaluated and have found to be responsible and effective stewards.

Our great need is for a renewed vision that will phase out ineffective and counterproductive government social programs and develop fresh approaches for churches and other community-based organizations to take the lead in fighting poverty. Some would contend that if the government would step aside, the faith community is waiting in the wings to take its rightful and responsible place. But realistically, most churches lack the capacity to care for their own flock, let alone the masses on the welfare rolls. The transformation to the Christian community taking responsibility for the poor and practicing responsible compassion will not happen overnight. It will require the federal government to maintain its safety-net programs while churches and faith-based organizations strengthen and expand their efforts to care for the "least of these." Together we can make a genuine and sustainable difference in the lives of the poor in America and around the globe.

18

AVOIDING
COMPASSION FATIGUE

In late December 2004, an enormous earthquake set off a giant tsunami in the Indian Ocean. It swept along the coasts, leaving a path of death and destruction, with the devastation particularly acute in Indonesia, Sri Lanka, India, and Thailand. In some coastal communities, waves reached 100 feet high. In the end, the tsunami was responsible for nearly 350,000 deaths and countless injuries. As images of human suffering filled our television screens, there was a global outpouring of prayer and financial donations to aid the victims. Experts estimate that as much as $7 billion was donated in the wake of the disaster—the largest and most widespread response in history.

The following year, Hurricane Katrina blew into New Orleans, Louisiana, breaching every levee and flooding about 80 percent of the city. At least 1836 people lost their lives in either the hurricane or the subsequent flooding. After a series of embarrassing miscues by government agencies, the American people once again gave money and resources to help the thousands of displaced families.

Undoubtedly the record financial donations from individuals and the thousands of volunteers were in part responses to the strong and widespread news coverage these events received. We watched the horror unfold on our television sets—images we won't soon forget—and we responded. The media should be applauded for giving these important stories a long shelf life beyond the typical media cycle. However, the media attention is a double-edged sword.

The 2004 tsunami killed 350,000 people.

With our 24-hour news channels reporting on various natural disasters, celebrities crusading against world poverty, and all the appeals for funds and images of suffering coming at us from nonprofit and relief organizations, we can't seem to avoid the multiplied stories of human misery. The pictures of thin and bloated African children whose tearful eyes are surrounded by flies, the film of devastated villages, the sound of sobbing and cries brought on by empty stomachs—we just can't seem to get away from them. And though we need to be aware of what is happening around us, sometimes it just feels like too much, and we are tempted to shut down. We suffer from overexposure, and overexposure is the prelude to "compassion fatigue."

Giving Fatigue

Compassion fatigue is the gradual lessening of compassion over time, usually due to a growing feeling that all the effort that is being expended is pointless. Compassion spurs us to get involved: to pray for the victims, volunteer hours at a local soup kitchen, participate in a mission trip, and give to help the homeless. But compassion fatigue sets in when we work and give...but begin to wonder why things don't seem to be getting better. We might feel as though all our best efforts are like trying to empty a swimming pool with a teaspoon. We grow weary from doing good after not seeing immediate results we'd hoped for. Eventually we can become callous and desensitized and no longer willing to hear another sad story or a charity's pitch for money.

Since the tsunami and Katrina, our nation and world have experienced disasters that prior to 2005 would have captured the headlines, but increasingly they only receive fleeting attention. Studies have shown that since 2005, a smaller percentage of people are willing to take note of a news story about a catastrophe or to read the report in a charity's newsletter. The sad result is that nonprofit organizations that offer disaster relief have found it increasingly difficult to raise the needed funds to provide aid. And recruiting volunteers to serve has become more of a challenge. The cries for help continue, but people are generally less willing to listen.

And we have grown more skeptical. We are more uncertain that our donations are going to be used wisely and as we intended. In the aftermath of the September 11 attacks, many charities set up funds for the families of victims of the terrorist attacks. They created public service announcements and sent out direct mail appeals for this purpose, and people responded generously. Then we learned that in some cases, a relatively small percentage of the donations actually made their way to the families. Donations were instead used to meet other general administrative needs. Even though one could argue that these were legitimate and needed long-term expenditures, many generous givers were left feeling as if they had been duped and cheated. Among Christians, reports continue of some religious leaders (I call them "panhandlers in suits") who raise enormous amounts of money in the name of compassion but absorb most of it for overhead or to support their elaborate lifestyles. These abuses make people more nervous and skeptical about giving. How this must grieve the Lord.

"Around the country, compassion fatigue is evident as people tire of seeing generosity misused or, apparently, of no use. As columnist Ellen Goodman noted, 'For many of us, there is a slow process by which...generosity can turn into resentment and sympathy can turn hard.'"[1] As Goodman notes, we can become not only fatigued but actually hardened against compassion. How sad that a handful of abusers are creating a scenario that is hurting all compassion organizations. For truly, most of the organizations are very responsible with the way they use their funds and are very transparent about how the money is being spent. Our response should not be to give up on giving, but instead to do some homework to make sure we are giving wisely. In appendix 4 of this book, you'll find a listing of organizations that are worthy of your support—nonprofits that are responsible and efficient and that operate with the highest values.

Weary from Doing Good

Much of what we have said so far is oriented to the fatigue that arises from overexposure and irresponsibility. But perhaps even more devastating is the compassion fatigue that arises in people who are giving their time and talent to be foot soldiers in the war against poverty and injustice—the people whose work as volunteers in food pantries, soup kitchens, homeless shelters, and other compassion ministries makes it possible for us to make strides against these problems. Sure, we critically need more donations…and we always will. But we also need those who will give of themselves to be *with* the poor.

Yet sometimes compassion in action can be so discouraging. As Mark Twain once wrote, "The cat, having sat upon a hot stove lid, will not sit upon a hot stove lid again. But he won't sit upon a cold stove lid either." When we have poured ourselves into a cause that fails to bear much fruit, we can become dispirited. We can be reluctant to try again. "Nothing is more disheartening than to invest enormous amounts of compassion and energy in counseling, treating, training, and connecting an addicted person, only to have him throw it away by returning to his destructive patterns."[2] Likewise, we can be so disappointed if we put a lot of time and labor into trying to correct a social injustice or to right an inequality, only to have things remain the same.

So whether cultural or personal, how can we avoid compassion fatigue or lessen its impact when it hits?

Plugging into the Power Source

Our best hope for dealing with compassion fatigue is to remember that God is our source. If we try to cope with all of the frustration and disappointment in our own strength and power, we are probably bound to fail and become discouragement's next victim. We need to experience God's heart and God's strength if we are to avoid compassion burnout. Prayer warrior Tommy Lofton told me a story about a father who was helping his son move into a college dorm and set up his room. While the father was unpacking some boxes of books and putting them on shelves, the son decided to hook up the computer. But when they tried to turn it on, nothing happened—a blank, dark screen. Trying to figure out what was wrong, the father crawled under the desk and discovered the problem: The power strip was plugged into itself!

If we are plugged into our own power supply, we are sure to experience compassion fatigue. We need to get plugged into God, the eternal source of wisdom, strength, joy, perspective, and compassion. Without Him to strengthen us, we cannot hope to keep ourselves focused and fueled to help others. We too quickly fall back on self-absorption, the desire for comfort, and the demand for short-term solutions. But God can help us take the spotlight off ourselves, offer us the courage to sacrifice, and give us a more patient and long-term eternal perspective on problems.

Plugging into God's resources doesn't mean that we can solve all the world's problems. That is unrealistic. Nor does it mean that we will be able to completely avoid getting tired or "weary in doing good." That is to be expected from time to time. But I believe we can avoid being overcome by compassion fatigue and losing our heart for helping if we remember that our strength is in God.

Convoy of Hope is not only faith-based but also based on faith—faith in God for its survival. At times finances have been rather thin, and sometimes the needed funds arrive only in the nick of time. But they have always arrived. We've learned that God is neither early nor late, but always on time. Many times we have clung to the scriptural promise, "My God will meet all your needs according to his glorious riches in Christ Jesus" (Philippians 4:19). He has always proven faithful and blessed us beyond imagination.

Over the years we have sometimes found ourselves running on empty both physically and economically...and then to our dismay, even emptier! These times never made sense to us because we were doing exactly what God has commanded His people to do—helping the poor—but sometimes it just felt hopeless. We would pray but just found ourselves feeling emptier. Now, looking back in the rearview mirror of life, we can see that God allowed us to become empty so He could fill us with His presence, provision, and power. And with His resources rather than ours, we were better prepared to expand His mission of reaching the lost and the least.

Filled with Emptiness

Since Convoy of Hope was founded in 1994, it has grown dramatically.

The expected growing pains have come with establishing an organization dedicated to improving the lives of the impoverished and hurting. Great faith has always been a requirement.

"At times we knew what it's like to have pressing needs and an empty warehouse," admits my brother Hal. "But during those times our faith in God's provision grew the greatest. On many occasions our leadership team gathered together and cried out to God, asking Him to open the storehouses of heaven so we could continue to help people."

One example, from early in Convoy's history, showed Hal how God would provide if the ministry remained faithful. Convoy desperately needed $53,000. Hal wrote his request on a Post-it note and then knelt in his office and prayed that God would provide. The next day a man stopped by the office and handed him a check for exactly $53,000.

God delights in filling empty containers. He loves to demonstrate His miraculous provision. When I speak of provision, I don't only mean financial blessings; I primarily mean His infusion of strength and wisdom and the way He uses others to support us and help us carry our load.

When a drought overtook the land in the time of Elijah, the prophet was sent by God to the aid of a widow who was literally down to her last meal for herself and her two sons. Surprisingly, Elijah asked this poor woman for bread and wine. She had to use her last drops of oil to make him a cake of bread. But when she obeyed his request, the miracle of multiplication began (1 Kings 17:15-16). As He did with this widow, God takes the little we have and makes a lot out of it! In a similar story from the life of Elisha (2 Kings 4), a widow was asked to gather all her jars of oil, as well as the empty jars of her neighbors. The woman already had empty jars, but God wanted more jars to fill! And He did.

Years ago I developed an association to assist President George W. Bush in the Faith-Based and Community Initiative. It was a step of faith because I believed that this could be a good program to expand outreach to the poor and needy by finding ways for the government and private organizations to cooperate. There really wasn't any money involved in the assignment, and I had only a "mustard seed" of funds to start this new venture. We sold most of our things and loaded what was left into our minivan to travel to our new home. When we arrived, we didn't immediately have money to purchase a home or rent a house, so we stayed in a hotel.

The very first morning in this new city, I awakened with an old song running in my mind: "Something Good Is Going to Happen to You." As I walked toward our vehicle (where we had stowed most of our belongings because the hotel room was pretty small) I wondered, *What miracle of God's provision is going to happen today?* I had a bounce in my step and joy in my heart that we were following the Lord in faith and on the cusp of something significant. Approaching the van, I saw a pile of glass glimmering in the morning sunshine. My heart sank. The back window had been smashed, and all of our possessions had been stolen.

Now, we had no money *and* no possessions.

I can't say that I wasn't angry and discouraged and disappointed. I was. But I chose to trust God to be my source. I had recently read the story about Elisha and the widow's jars. Out of the abundance of God's blessings the woman had been able to feed her family and even sell some of the oil to pay her debts. In the same way God began to fill our empty van, empty bank account, shallow faith, and meager vision with His abundance.

First, the hotel, which was undergoing a major renovation, decided to give us a lot of really beautiful furniture that was being replaced. It was ten times nicer than what we had before. Then donations for this new endeavor began to flow in from people I had just recently met or never even knew. Within four months I was hosting the first of many gatherings at the White House for faith-based leaders. A new chapter of service was opened in my life. In retrospect, something good *did* begin to happen to me on that day of disappointment and frustration.

Obedience, Not Outcomes

If we are going to avoid compassion fatigue, we must leave the final outcome to God. I am reminded of the story of Jonah. God had given him a big mission: "Go to the great city of Nineveh and preach against it, because its wickedness has come up before me" (Jonah 1:2). This was a tall order, for the people of this city were famous for their debauchery and moral laxity. Idol worship was the primary religion, not worship of the living God. I don't believe that Jonah really imagined that he would be able to make much of an impact. After a false start and a ride in the belly of a big fish, Jonah arrived in Nineveh, where he preached a message of the need for repentance.

Surprisingly, the people of Nineveh listened. Their hearts were changed, and they repented of their evil. Jonah's ministry bore fruit, and God felt compassion for the formerly wayward nation. This ticked Jonah off. He thought his mission was to be one of announcing judgment. But instead, God was forgiving the evildoers. When Jonah expressed his frustration to God, the Lord said to him, "Have you any right to be angry?" In other words, "Do your mission and leave the outcome to Me!"

We all want to see the fruits of our labor, and we can feel debilitated when results do not appear as we envision or within the expected time frame. We are tempted to be angry or give up or look for someone to blame. But God says to us what He essentially said to Jonah: "Do your mission and leave the outcome to Me." When we leave the outcome to God, the success of our work is determined not by results, but by our obedience. That takes off a lot of the pressure and should help us to stay at our task. Our job is to serve, and God—in His own time—will bring about the results.

Regardless of what the immediate failures and setbacks might be, we must believe that there is always hope. When we give up hope, we lose our effectiveness. To keep our hope alive, we may need a new way of looking at the situation, a new paradigm.

He's in Your Boat

A paradigm is the lens through which we interpret events and develop our opinions. Our paradigms are formed by our past experiences, knowledge, and beliefs. New information can cause us to change our paradigms—what we call a "paradigm shift."

A young man with a brand-new sports car decided to take it out for a spin. As he sped down a country road with the top down on his stylish convertible, he saw a woman coming toward him in the opposite lane. She put her head out her window and yelled, "Pig!" He was shocked. What right did she have to call him a pig? He was minding his own business, and he wasn't going that fast. The more he thought about it, the angrier he became. He pressed down on the gas pedal, and as he rounded a corner...he hit the pig.

A paradigm shift had occurred. From his vantage point the woman was rude for calling him a pig. But the new information he received from the crushed hood of his car changed his opinion of the woman. She had been trying to warn him.

If we see from a limited earthly perspective, we can easily lose hope. We need a paradigm shift. We need to see a bigger picture, as the disciples did when they were in a boat with Jesus out in the middle of the Sea of Galilee and a huge storm began to rage about them. The waves were splashing over the side of the boat as it was violently tossed about on the sea, and the disciples began to fear for their lives. "Lord, save us!" they yelled. "We're going to drown!" (Matthew 8:25) From their paradigm, the situation looked hopeless. The sea was extremely rough, they were far from land, and...well, human beings can't breathe underwater.

The one thing they did right was to rouse Jesus, who was asleep in the stern, seemingly oblivious to the tumult. Jesus stood and spoke the word *peace*, and suddenly everything was calm. When they cried out for Jesus, they connected with the one who could give them hope—and give them a solution to their struggle.

We can overcome the storms in our lives—fear, disappointment, burnout—when we acknowledge the one who is in the boat with us. When we see others who are depressed and defeated, we can remind them of the other passenger in their boat, the Prince of Peace. We need hope, and we need to be reminded and to be a reminder to others that we have a new paradigm, a new perspective because of Jesus.

The apostle Paul knew how to keep going in the face of the gravest difficulties. He had been whipped and beaten and imprisoned and shipwrecked for the sake of his calling. But he didn't give up. Instead, as he writes in 2 Corinthians 4:8-9, "We are hard pressed on every side, but not crushed; perplexed, but not in despair; persecuted, but not abandoned; struck down but not destroyed." Among all his other trials, I'm sure Paul felt the same pains that a compassion revolutionary feels. Sometimes all his efforts appeared to achieve very little. But he never lost hope because he never lost perspective.

WHAT CAN I DO? SOME PRACTICAL WAYS TO MAKE A DIFFERENCE...

- Find out what breaks God's heart, and pray that it will break your heart too.

- Ask God to refresh and renew your commitment to giving and serving others.

- Determine to persevere regardless of setbacks, slow progress, or weariness.

Keep Swinging the Bat!

"Donaldson, you're next at bat!" barked my coach. As I walked out of the dugout, my throat went dry, my heart began to pound, my knees shook, and beads of nervous sweat formed on my forehead. The game, the season, and the championship hung in the balance. So did my standing with my teammates. If I struck out—which, based on my history, was not unlikely—we lose. Simple as that.

I heard someone in the dugout ask in a panicked whine, "Donaldson's up?" The coach's affirmative response was met by a chorus of moans and was the cue for the bat boy to begin to gather our equipment. I looked up into the stands to try to spot my mother, but I couldn't see her because too many people were standing in preparation to exit. I think they just couldn't take the pain of watching me strike out again.

But I was determined to prove them wrong.

Earlier that year I had been promoted to the higher level in Little League, but I was about a foot shorter than most of the other players and as skinny as a Louisville Slugger bat. Even the smallest uniform looked more like a tent on my thin frame. I wore the number 11, and when I tucked in my shirt, it looked like I was wearing suspenders. When I tightened my belt, the back pockets connected into one big smile. Fortunately, my duties were pretty much limited to sitting on the bench.

During one game I was sent into right field after one of our players got hurt. Taking my place deep in right field I prayed that the ball would not be hit to me. Sure enough, the first batter up hit a grounder to our second baseman, who watched it go through his legs and continue hopping toward me. Approaching the ball, I could see the runner decide to try to turn a single into a double, probably thinking this was his chance since there was an untested rookie in right field. I scooped up the ball and threw it with all my might toward second base, where the umpire was waiting to make the call. My errant throw didn't make it to the second baseman. Instead it hit the umpire in the side of the head and knocked him out cold.

As they carried the umpire off the field, I headed for the dugout, where I angrily slammed my glove down on the bench and told the coach, "I quit! I can't do anything right! I quit!"

My coach walked over, put his hand on my shoulder and told me, "Donaldson, you can't quit. You are part of a team. If you quit, then I guess we should all quit." I thought he was bluffing until he started walking over to the other umpire—the one who was still conscious. I had no choice. I ran back out on the field and resumed my position. It was an important lesson that had prepared me for this moment of truth.

So here we were at the championship game, the last inning. The bases were loaded with two outs...and I was up to bat. The game, the season, and the championship hung in the balance.

Looking over at the pitcher, I had to avert my eyes. He looked like Goliath wearing a baseball cap. The coach pulled me aside for a little pep talk. He grabbed both my shoulders, looked me in the eye and said, "Donaldson, I know you are scared. But if you will just stay in the batter's box and swing with all your might, then in my eyes you are successful...regardless of what happens."

I took my place at the plate and repeated his words under my breath. *All I have to do is stay in the batter's box and swing the bat, and I am successful. I can do that.*

The pitcher threw the first pitch: ball one.

The second pitch was another ball.

I didn't swing at the third pitch and the umpire called it a strike.

The next pitch was in the same area. I took a mighty swing and missed.

The count was now two balls, two strikes. Now it was all on the line. I looked up at Goliath and said to myself, *Well, if I'm going to go out, I might as well go out swinging.* The pitcher wound up and threw the ball right down the middle of the plate. I swung as hard as I could and heard a loud ping echo across the baseball field.

Looking up, I could not spot the ball, so I thought it had hooked foul. But someone yelled, "RUN! RUN!" so I darted toward first base and then onto second base as something strange happened. My teammates emptied out of the dugout and were running across the baseball diamond toward me. They were jumping up and down in jubilation. Moments later I was at the bottom of a dog pile asking a fellow teammate, "What happened?"

"Donaldson, you did it! You hit a grand slam! We won!"

When you are serving others, there will doubtless be times that you will feel like quitting. You will give it your best, only to strike out. But be assured that if you just stay with it, just stay in the game, there will be times of jubilation and celebration as you see God use you in amazing ways. At the end of the game of life, what really matters is that we stayed in the batter's box and kept swinging with all our might. If we do that each and every day, in God's eyes *we are successful*!

19

FROM WOUNDED
TO WOUNDED HEALER

My mother never really developed culinary skills. Her specialty was Hamburger Helper...without the hamburger. Her yam casserole was a concoction of yams and marshmallows that floated like icebergs on a particularly unappetizing gooey orange ocean. I sometimes joked with her that she used the smoke alarm as her oven timer. Or that I am living proof of Jesus' promise at the end of Mark's Gospel: "When they drink deadly poison, it will not hurt them at all." Just to be on the safe side, my siblings and I prayed before *and after* each meal.

Mom knew she wasn't a great cook, but that didn't keep her from inviting people over for dinner, especially widows or single mothers or the lonely. Her meals were part of her ministry. Despite the tragic death of her husband, multiple surgeries, and years of having to fend for herself, she reached out to others. What she lacked as a cook she more than made up for with her hospitality.

Sometimes we excuse ourselves from reaching out to others because we have our own problems and challenges. But God isn't looking for perfect people to do His work. He is looking for the wounded to become wounded healers.

The time we have spent in life's valleys make our mountaintops more authentic to others. Our testimony of overcoming failure and obstacles will capture the attention of our world. A friend of mine who is a chiropractor once shared that he didn't spend a dime on advertising his services. "So how do you acquire new clients?" I asked him.

He smiled. "My clients share with their friends how much pain they were

in before the treatment and how good they felt once I had worked on them...
and that's all the marketing I need." Isn't that God's strategy for meeting
the needs of the world—that we who have been healed spiritually, physically,
and emotionally can become God's instruments of healing?

Keep Your Smile

My grandmother (Gram, we called her) was probably the biggest single
influence on my life. She graced the world with a seemingly unshakable smile
and was one of the wittiest people I ever met. From her unwaveringly positive
outlook, you'd never guess that two husbands had cheated on her and then
abandoned her with little to live on. You'd never expect such unflagging joy
from someone who battled such severe arthritis that it permanently bowed
her back and made it nearly impossible to walk. Despite all this heartache and
excruciating pain, her motto was, "Honey, don't let anyone steal your smile."

As her condition worsened, we eventually had to admit her to a senior
care facility, where she could receive professional care around the clock. After
moving her in and getting some of her stuff settled, I wheeled her down to the
dining hall. I could tell she was taken aback by what she saw—a large group of
residents were seated in a semicircle around the table, but there was not a bit of
conversation. Most of them just stared down at their food, carefully avoiding
eye contact with the others while scooping the food into their mouths. The
whole scene was so depressing that I couldn't really figure out what to say. But
she found words: "Honey, I have my work cut out for me, don't I?"

She saw the challenge as an opportunity.

Weeks later I paid a visit after returning from a lengthy trip overseas.
She wasn't in her room, but I could hear noise coming from the dining hall.
Curious, I entered the dining room only to discover a bunch of senior citizens acting more like wild teenagers. Most of them were talking, laughing,
smiling, and joking. Of course, the life of the party was Gram! It was hard
to believe this was the same place I had visited just a few weeks earlier. The
whole atmosphere had been changed by an elderly woman, hunched over by
disease, who decided she would make a difference. She declared, "I refuse
to be a victim when I can live a victorious life for myself and others!"

Keep Your Focus

Much is determined by what we decide to focus on. Race car drivers
will tell you that when they are speeding along at 200 miles an hour and
see debris on the track, the worst thing they can do is to focus on the object.

That often leads to a collision with the very thing they want to avoid. Instead, they look away and stay focused on the road ahead of them. And so in life, what you focus on is what you will become. What you dwell on will determine your destiny. If you decide that your own woundedness exempts you from reaching out to others, you will only reinforce the damage done to you. If you decide to let your wounds become a motivation for healing for others, you will find joy and deeper healing for yourself.

In 1 Kings 18, the prophet Elijah finds himself up on Mount Carmel in a competition with the false prophets of the pagan idols. When Elijah calls down fire from God, the altar of Baal is consumed. We can hardly imagine a more powerful demonstration of God's reality and strength. And yet...

In the very next chapter we find Elijah so depressed that he just wants to pull away from all the struggles of life and give up. In the space of one chapter he has gone from feeling like a spiritual hero to feeling like a zero. What had happened? Well, first there was a famine in the land. Second, because of what he had done before, the people expected him to solve the problem. And third, the wicked Queen Jezebel wanted him dead for ridiculing her religious beliefs and killing her false prophets on Mount Carmel.

The Bible tells us that "Elijah was afraid and ran for his life." He finally came to a desolate place, where he sat beneath a tree and "prayed that he might die" (1 Kings 19:3-4). However, God was not finished with Elijah. He told him to get up, go out, and go back. This is good advice for wounded healers who want to keep working for the Lord.

Get Up! (1 Kings 19:5)

Sometimes the most spiritual thing you can do is simply to get up. Sometimes that is easier said than done. It must have felt that way to Elijah, because God had to repeat the command a second time—"Get up!"

The National Football League seems to keep statistics on everything. One of the more recent things they have started to track is YAC (yards after contact). When the quarterback hands the football to the running back, the back is almost always going to be hit by a defensive player who is trying to tackle him. Occasionally a player will run to a touchdown without being touched, but that is pretty rare. Normally he gets hit at least once before he goes down. The best running backs are those who can be hit multiple times and still remain on their feet. So statisticians calculate how many yards backs gain from the point of initial contact until they are actually tackled.

None of us are immune from contact with problems, pressures, and difficult people. The question becomes, what do we do after facing multiple hits from life? Wounded healers are people who have a lot of YAC—yards after contact. And when they are down, they don't stay down. They get up and press forward in life.

God is able to use every hit we take and every wound we receive to mold us and shape our ability to help others. These kinds of trials build our faith. "Consider it pure joy, my brothers, whenever you face trials of many kinds, because you know that the testing of your faith develops perseverance. Perseverance must finish its work so that you may be mature and complete, not lacking anything" (James 1:2-4).

Go Out! (1 Kings 19:11)

Elijah was hiding out, nursing his pain, and cursing his fate. When we are wounded, our natural tendency is to go and hide, to protect ourselves from further pain. But hiding from God and hiding from our church family puts us in a dangerous place. Extended isolation is never a good thing. In isolation we are open to all kinds of temptations and spiritual dangers (1 Peter 5:8). And one of the enemy's most effective strategies is to entice us to wallow in self-pity. Self-pity comes from a combination of feeling victimized (*somebody did this to me*) and feeling like a failure. When Elijah was experiencing this insecurity, God told him to get out of the cave, so Elijah crawled out once again to fight the good fight.

But first, God wanted to give Elijah an experience of His presence. He needed to get beyond his self-pity if he was really to experience God in all His quiet majesty. Sometimes when we are wounded, the last thing we really want is the presence of God. But only in His presence will we find safety, restoration, and renewed strength for our journey.

We may think that time will heal our wounds, but it really doesn't. Our memories of pain remain with us. I can still remember as a child hearing my grieving mother weeping at night in her bedroom. It tore at my heart until I felt I could hardly stand it. Has the pain of such memories ever disappeared? Not for me. When I think of those days, I still feel the anger, hurt, and sorrow swelling up inside me. But I chose not to let pain and self-pity write the story of my life. I chose to "get up," "get out," and find my inner peace and strength from the presence of the Lord. So much of our happiness is based on our choices. Abraham Lincoln wisely noted, "Most people are about as happy as they choose to be."

Jesus drew a clear distinction between what the enemy desires for us and what God desires for us: "The thief comes only to steal and kill and destroy; I have come that they may have life, and have it to the full" (John 10:10). Wounded healers refuse to allow the enemy to rob them of the great gift that God offers—living life to the fullest.

Go Back! (1 Kings 19:15)

When we try to run away from our pain, God has a way of returning us to the place where it started so we can deal with it. That is what God had in store for Elijah. He had to go back to the very basics to find the comfort God wanted to provide. He didn't hear God in the powerful wind, or the earthquake, or the fire—none of these big dramatic events. He heard God in the quiet of a "still small voice."

Hurting people often hurt others without even realizing it. Over the years I have observed that unless people enter a conscious and determined path to healing, they are vulnerable to damaging others—an infection of woundedness that spreads from us to those around us. Because wounded people tend to focus on their pain, ruminating over past hurts and failures, their bitterness and inward abuse can sometimes surface in harmful attitudes and words and actions toward other people.

The path from wounded to wounded healer begins with changing the way we talk to ourselves. Paul shows us the way: "Finally, brothers, whatever is true, whatever is noble, whatever is right, whatever is pure, whatever is lovely, whatever is admirable—if anything is excellent or praiseworthy—think about such things" (Philippians 4:8). Instead of focusing on our pain, we need to focus on what God is doing in us to heal the pain. That is the first step toward becoming one who spreads peace and joy rather than pain and negativity.

Then we have to be ready to walk the path that leads us from being one of the wounded into becoming a wounded healer. I think the steps along this path can be best summarized as grieving, gathering, and giving. Let's see how these can turn the wounds of our lives into places of healing.

Wounded to Wounded Healer

First, we must allow ourselves to *grieve*. It isn't healthy to just pretend that nothing has happened or to try to plaster on a false smile. Grief is a natural, healthy process that God uses to help us recover from emotional pain. As the English hymn writer William Cowper once wrote, "Grief is itself medicine." We should not feel guilty about grieving over the painful things we experience because it is part of God's pathway to healing. There is nothing unspiritual about grieving. Remember that at Lazarus's tomb, Jesus wept. As Isaiah reminds us, He is "a Man of sorrows and acquainted with grief" (Isaiah 53:3 NKJV).

Part of the process of grieving is to *gather*. We need the comfort of family and friends, the love and encouragement of those closest to us. Like Elijah, we can be tempted to draw away. We may need a bit of solitude, but soon we need to gather back together with those we love and with our brothers and sisters in Christ. The writer of Hebrews reminds us of the necessity of gathering, especially in the most difficult of times: "Let us not give up meeting together, as some are in the habit of doing, but let us encourage one another—and all the more as you see the Day approaching" (Hebrews 10:25).

Most importantly, we need to continue to *give*. Giving out of our own sorrow brings healing and comfort to others. Paul writes, "Blessed be the God...of all comfort, who comforts us in all our tribulation, that we may be able to comfort those who are in any trouble, with the comfort with which we ourselves are comforted by God" (2 Corinthians 1:3-4).

Healing Through Helping

Healing can be found in serving. Wounds may last a lifetime, but at some point the grieving needs to end and the giving needs to begin. Ecclesiastes 3:1,4 tells us, "To everything there is a season, a time for every purpose under heaven...a time to weep, and a time to laugh; a time to mourn, and a time to dance." When we begin to give of ourselves to others, our focus shifts from ourselves to them. Self-pity gets crowded out, and our problems grow strangely dim.

One of my pastor friends told me a story about a woman in his congregation named Linda. She was constantly setting up appointments to come in for counseling, but the pastor saw very little improvement in her emotional state. Session after session seemed to do little good for her. One day he was looking for a volunteer to assist some children whose mother was in the hospital. Linda happened to be in for yet another appointment, so he decided to ask her if she'd be willing to help. She seemed very reluctant, but finally agreed...as long as it didn't get in the way of her counseling appointments.

A few weeks passed, and Linda hadn't called to set up an appointment. The pastor grew concerned. So when he spotted her at the Sunday service with the children, he pulled her aside. "How are you doing?" he inquired. "I noticed that you didn't schedule a counseling appointment for the past few weeks."

"Pastor," she responded, "I don't have time to meet with you. After feeding these children and taking them to school and chaperoning them to other activities, there isn't any time left." Then she smiled, and he saw that a healing had occurred in her that months of counseling had not been able to achieve.

God does not waste anything in our lives. He uses everything that happens to us. There's a story about a man who became stranded on a deserted island. Each and every day he spent hours by the water's edge, looking for passing ships that he could signal and thus be rescued. Weeks passed like this, and he never spotted a ship. He became deeply discouraged and wondered if he would be trapped on the island for the rest of his life. With heavy heart he decided he needed to build a more permanent shelter, so he chose a place perched on an overlook about a half a mile from the shore. After weeks of intense labor, his new home—made of bamboo and palm leaves—was finally finished. He continued to check the horizon for a passing vessel but always in vain.

Eventually he figured out ways to make himself a little more comfortable, and he learned out how to start a fire and keep it going. But his sadness and loneliness grew. One day, he was building a fire when a blustery wind blew in from the south and swept the fire against the walls of his home. It was dry, so the flame quickly spread over the house. He tried in vain to extinguish the inferno, but it was no use.

Overcome with grief, he collapsed to the ground and sobbed uncontrollably.

But then he heard the unmistakable sound of a ship's horn. Scrambling to his feet, he fled down to the water's edge, where he saw a ship approaching in the distance. Not wanting to take any chance of missing it, he plunged into the water and swam out to the vessel.

Once aboard, the captain greeted him. "Welcome aboard!"

Though almost lost for words, the castaway managed to ask, "How did you find me? How did you know I was here?"

The captain grinned and replied, "We saw your smoke signal."

God has a way of using even the most terrible experiences of our lives to teach us patience (with others and ourselves), to strengthen us, to make us more sympathetic and caring, and to increase our ability and desire to show compassion. The challenges of your life could very well be the smoke signals God will use to bless you and to bless others through you. Rick Warren reminds us, "God loves to bring good out of bad. He loves to turn crucifixions into resurrections. Every obstacle is an opportunity. Every problem has potential. Every crisis is an opportunity for ministry. Every hurt God wants to use for His glory."

A Twist of Faith

Anne Beiler's life went into a tailspin after her 19-month-old daughter was run over by a farm tractor and killed in 1975. Anne, in her mid twenties at the time, found herself depressed and on the brink of suicide. Despite being a faithful churchgoer, she didn't feel she could share her pain with friends or family members.

Anne and her husband, Jonas, whom she had wed at 19, drifted apart. The couple didn't talk about the tragedy and its ramifications. Instead, they remained silent partners who simply lived together. She even became involved with another man.

Seven years into the ordeal, Jonas convinced his wife to go with him to marriage counseling at their church. "I really didn't want to go, even though my life was falling apart," Anne says. "But I had a breakthrough, and God started dealing with me." And the Lord began to restore their marriage.

Anne needed to find a way to make ends meet in those early years, and she remembered how much she loved baking while growing up on an Amish-Mennonite farm with seven siblings. Because Anne had asthma as a child, she didn't venture outside much, so she became the cook and baker for the family. By age 12, Anne made up to 70 pies and cakes from scratch each week to sell at a nearby farmer's market. She didn't skimp on ingredients and always carefully made sure the food looked and tasted great.

"God often uses our history to fulfill His plan," Anne says. "God was preparing me for the future." After reconciling with her husband, Anne bought a concession stand at a busy farmers' market in Downington, Pennsylvania. She sold everything from pizza to ice cream, but customers gobbled up the hand-rolled soft pretzels the fastest. Because of the demand, Anne eventually dropped the rest of the product line and concentrated on pretzels.

From that modest start, she has become one of the nation's leading entrepreneurs. Auntie Anne's Hand-Rolled Soft Pretzels raked in $236 million in sales in 2003. In 15 years, the company has grown from a single outlet in Lancaster, Pennsylvania, to more than 1000 locations worldwide, with a workforce of more than 10,000. Auntie Anne's, headquartered in Gap, Pennsylvania, has found a niche among snack-seeking mall shoppers. The company doesn't advertise, but pretty much everyone has seen—or smelled—those tasty pretzels.

Jonas and Anne Beiler, founders of Auntie Anne's.

More recently, Anne and her husband sold the business and launched a powerful compassion ministry that has changed the lives of countless individuals through counseling and the meeting of practical needs at the Gap Family Center. I talked with Anne about her journey:

DAVE: You built a multimillion-dollar enterprise from scratch. Employees, customers, and industry analysts marveled at how a woman without a high school education, business knowledge, or financial capital could form the largest soft pretzel chain in the country. But tell us how you traveled a path from being wounded to becoming a wounded healer.

ANNE: When our daughter Angie was run over by a farm tractor, I acted on the outside as though I had dealt victoriously with the tragedy, but bitterness, guilt, and depression consumed me. I didn't allow myself to grieve and confided in no one. Then a minister offered to provide a listening ear, but he had other motives besides my mental health. He seduced me, and I experienced an unhealthy transference of emotions that turned into six years of sexual abuse.

DAVE: How did that make you feel inside?

ANNE: I hated myself. I wanted to self-destruct, but I held to a promise in Malachi 3:11: "I will prevent pests from devouring your crops, and the vines in your fields will not cast their fruit."

DAVE: Where did you finally receive help?

ANNE: I never stopped attending church, even though many times I didn't want to go. We have been taught in church that some sins, like gossip, are more acceptable than others. When it comes to sexual sins, we can't confess them openly because to some people they are unpardonable. Only after counseling sessions with EMERGE Ministries founder Dr. Richard Dobbins did I grasp the value of preserving my faith, my family, and indeed my life. The power of confession transformed my life. I felt like a new person, without shame and guilt. I'm overawed by God's absolute love.

DAVE: How can the church open its arms to broken people?

ANNE: Many withdraw from church because they already are berating themselves and can't take having more guilt heaped upon them. What we really need is to have arms extended to us that say, "I know what you've done, but I love you and forgive you anyway." The sin doesn't need to be accepted, but the church needs to follow the model of Jesus and love people who are broken. That's what Jesus did best.

DAVE: How did this experience lead you and Jonas to begin the Gap Family Center?

ANNE: We sold Auntie Anne's in 2005. It has been my husband's vision for more than 20 years to build what you have called a "shopping mall of compassion." Jonas likes to say, "You can't keep sweeping things under the rug and ignoring them...the problems won't just go away." We wanted to pull together the people and resources to help family causes flourish in every way. When my husband found out about my sin, instead of judging, condemning, and criticizing me, he granted mercy. If the church will do that, there is no limit to the number of people that will take the journey of hope and healing.

Out of tragedy, sadness, and sin, a powerful ministry of compassion was birthed for the Beilers. Does this mean that God has erased all their painful memories? Of course not. But He has turned their woundedness into a heart of healing for many broken lives.

WHAT CAN I DO? SOME PRACTICAL WAYS TO MAKE A DIFFERENCE...

- Submit your past hurts or failures to God and believe for complete healing.
- If you are suffering from a wound, follow the biblical pattern of grieving, gathering, and giving.
- Be sensitive to someone's pain today and consider ways to be an encouragement.

Crooked Toes

Fragments of our painful past can remind us of God's power and His purpose for our lives. The apostle Paul endured an affliction he referred to as his thorn in the flesh, which he said God allowed because His power is made perfect in weakness (2 Corinthians 12:7-10). For me it is crooked toes.

Just days after my father was killed, my Uncle Jack came to visit. "Is *that* what you are going to wear to school?" he said, casting a woeful eye over my clothing.

"This is all I have," I had to admit, embarrassed. I only had a couple of changes of clothing to my name. We had little money for such luxuries as new clothes.

Uncle Jack opened his wallet and pulled out a wad of bills, which he handed to Gram. "Take the boys out and buy them some new clothes for school."

I still remember the feeling of swelling pride as I walked out of the store wearing brand-new pants, shirt, and shoes. The shoes were the shiniest, sharpest-looking black shoes I had ever seen. And now they were mine. Mom called them my church shoes, but I wore them for almost every occasion.

Over time I noticed that it got increasingly difficult to slip the shoes on. I'd have to work at it because my feet continued to grow. When I jammed my feet into them and wore them for a few hours, my toes cramped up for lack of space. But I never said anything to Mom because I loved those shoes, and I knew she couldn't afford to buy me new ones anyway.

The result was that my toes began to curl in to accommodate the limited room. It wasn't easy to hide my crooked toes from my family and friends, and if anyone happened to notice, I just made up a story. "This is how I was born, but the doctor said my toes will straighten out soon."

During my teenage years, most of my toes eventually did straighten out, but to this day my little toe and its partner on each foot remain curled and a bit deformed. A friend recommended that I go to an orthopedic surgeon and have the toes surgically straightened, but I probably never will. My toes are tied to God's calling on my life. When I wake up in the morning and put on my socks and shoes, I look down at my ugly, deformed toes, and I am reminded of the countless children around the globe who have crooked toes, stomachs bloated from hunger, or bodies wasting away from diseases.

In one way or another we all have crooked toes—wounds that were self-inflicted or the result of difficulties of life draining the passion out of us. The big question is, what are we going to do about our crooked toes? Are we going to settle with feeling sorry for ourselves? Or will we allow ourselves to be moved with compassion for others? Keep in mind the words of the apostle Paul:

> Therefore we do not lose heart. Though outwardly we are wasting away, yet inwardly we are being renewed day by day. For our light and momentary troubles are achieving for us eternal glory that far outweighs them all. So we fix our eyes not on what is seen, but on what is unseen. For what is seen is temporary, but what is unseen is eternal (2 Corinthians 4:16-18).

Our wounded world is waiting for wounded healers.

20

A DECLARATION
OF COMPASSION

Every successful revolution has a clearly articulated reason for needing to overthrow the status quo. Thomas Jefferson, for example, penned the Declaration of Independence as a statement of what the American Revolution was all about. It contained the ideas, beliefs, and commitments that rallied people to the revolution, and it inspired those who had been content sitting on the sidelines to get personally involved. Perhaps we revolutionaries of compassion need a similar declaration of our goals, purposes, and commitments in the fight against poverty, sickness, disease, and economic injustice. We need to say, "To consign other human beings to living in squalor, need, and despair is unacceptable."

My own version of such a Declaration of Compassion is a work in progress. I offer it not as a definitive statement, but as a starting point for compassion revolutionaries as they think about the problems we face and how we can begin taking action for real change. I offer seven characteristics or qualities of compassion revolutionaries. Perhaps you can use this as a checklist to evaluate your personal commitment to the cause of compassion.

Declaration 1

Compassion revolutionaries become aware of the depth and immensity of the needs of others.

The level of need can seem overwhelming when we look honestly at the state of things. We can feel sad, angry, depressed, or defeated when we seriously contemplate the immensity of the problems that face so many in our world. No wonder we naturally tend to turn away, to avert our eyes from such distressing realities. But that doesn't make the problems go away.

It takes courage to be compassion revolutionaries, to open our hearts and minds to uncomfortable truths about the state of our world. But we cannot hope to solve problems just by wishing they didn't exist. Ignoring them doesn't make them go away. We may force the picture of a starving child out of our minds, but that doesn't change the fact that countless children are in that very condition right now.

The ugly truths about human suffering are rarely seen on the slick covers of magazines or on the front pages of newspapers. And when they do become headline news, they are soon shuffled off to the back pages. Just this morning I read an important article on the rapid growth of world hunger. It was not on the front page, but rather tucked away on page 7A, where only the diligent were likely to find it. The truth is, a lot of people just don't want to know. Reality overwhelms them.

But compassion revolutionaries cannot afford to ignore the truth. We know that change will come only as our awareness is raised. We may need to work to get up to speed on the issues. We might need to read the newspaper a little more carefully and pay attention to the problems relegated to the back pages. We might need to read the fine little magazines put out by World Vision, Convoy of Hope, and others. We might need to read one of the many excellent books on poverty issues or the stories of missionaries who have given their lives to spread not only the good news of Jesus but also practical medical and relief aid.

Many churches organize short-term mission opportunities to help people open their eyes to the world around them. Picking up a hammer to build a home or passing out medicine provides an experience of living among the needy. Once you have experienced this, you can no longer treat the problem as an abstraction, for you have seen the faces of those in need. You have talked with them, laughed with them, and shared a meal with them. You realize that despite our many surface differences, we are all really very much alike, and we share many of the same hopes and dreams for ourselves and for our children.

Traveling a long distance to help others can be a wonderful experience for those who are able, but it is not the only way to begin recognizing the needs of others. You can become more aware by simply paying closer attention to the problems around your own neighborhood, looking for ways that you can reach out and make a difference in someone's life.

In order to become more aware of others' needs, we must allow our hearts to become more vulnerable, to let them break over human suffering and hopelessness. As we begin to feel something of God's compassion toward the hurting, we will no longer be able to turn our eyes away and ignore the pain.

Most of us tend to think of ourselves as being compassionate. We believe that we are kindhearted and empathetic toward human suffering. But this begs the question, if so many of us are compassionate, why do so many fellow humans go to bed hungry, shiver through the night from inadequate housing, and awaken to face another day of suffering from preventable diseases?

Sometimes we Christians become so focused on salvation—on getting souls into heaven—that we forget that people can hardly hear God's words of hope when their stomachs are rumbling from hunger. We want to get them to the altar to commit themselves to Jesus, but we fall short of caring for them as whole people—people with very tangible needs. Would not our words, so often rejected out of hand, carry more weight if they were propped up by compassionate actions?

We rightly talk about a God of love and caring and compassion, and we have experienced these very things in our lives. But are we willing to allow our own hearts to be broken over the suffering of others, to be vulnerable enough to help them carry the weight of their pain as much as is possible for us?

Perhaps we should ask of God what Mother Teresa asked: "May God break my heart so completely that the whole world falls in."

Declaration 2

Compassion revolutionaries recognize the biblical imperative to care for the needs of "the least of these."

Many Christians mistakenly assume that the Bible is concerned only with spiritual matters (like salvation, prayer, and theology) and moral issues (like sexual sins, murder, and stealing). But that is simply not true. The Bible is the most holistic document ever written. It addresses just about every area of human existence and every issue we can imagine, including family, education, health, finances, taxes, equal rights, the environment, social justice, and yes, poverty. In fact, the amount of space in the Bible dedicated to discussing the plight of the poor is overwhelming and, to many Christians, surprising. This theme is not just mentioned in a verse or two, but runs throughout every section of the Old and New Testaments. If we desire to be biblical Christians, we should care about what God cares about. And the Bible makes abundantly clear that God cares deeply about the poor, the destitute, and the needy.

I once heard a Bible scholar say, "When you read the Bible, what you focus on determines what you miss." In other words, God's Word has so much to say that we can easily miss important themes because we are so focused on other themes. That is one good argument for reading the Bible again and again throughout our lives. We will always find something new! That is part of the miracle of the Scriptures. But many Christians tend to focus so much on devotional themes that they miss what the Bible has to say about those in need. They gloss over the passages that reveal the huge priority this issue was to have in covenant people's lives. We can easily overlook how much emphasis God placed on compassion for the poor, the homeless, the helpless, the left out, and the alienated.

When you read the Bible with your eyes open to this issue, you might be amazed to find that it is one of the most central themes in all of Scripture. More than 2100 verses related to poverty and economic injustice are scattered throughout the Old and New Testaments. The topic doesn't just pop up in a random discussion here and there. It is a prevalent theme you can trace through the entirety of Scripture.

Jim Wallis did an experiment while a seminary student. He asked some other students to mark every Bible passage that mentioned poverty and economic injustice. Then he and the others cut these passages out of the Bible. The students dutifully fell to the task, scissors in hand, examining every verse of the Bible and removing every mention of either topic. When the experiment was complete, Jim held aloft the Bible that had been stripped of these important themes. It was a tattered mess, gutted of pages and partial pages all the way through. It was a very powerful visual demonstration of just how common this theme is throughout the Scriptures.

In appendix 1 you'll find a survey of what the Bible has to say about this issue. I hope you'll take the time to explore that information and take to heart God's perspective on poverty and economic injustice.

Declaration 3

Compassion revolutionaries challenge the perception that the problem is too big to be fixed, and they catch the vision of being the hands and feet of Jesus.

The exposure to human misery can be so overwhelming that it paralyzes some people from doing anything. They may think, *I can't do anything about it, so it is not my responsibility.*

In a conversation with a Christian leader, I made a comment about the need for more societal commitment to the problem of poverty. He shook his head, mumbled something about the fear of higher taxes, and went on to quote Jesus to justify the existence of poverty: "The poor you will always have with you." This bothered me deeply. Regardless of how we feel about government programs and taxes, we should be saddened when people use Jesus' words about the pervasiveness of poverty as an excuse to not do anything about it.

In his book *The Hole in Our Gospel*, Rich Stearns writes, "The world's problems just seem too big and too hard for most of us; it's so much easier to retreat from them than to take them on. On Sunday morning, safe in our church pews and surrounded by friends, it can be all too easy to leave the world's violence, suffering, and turmoil outside—out of sight, out of mind."[1] As we have seen throughout this book, the problems are not insoluble—they are just big and difficult. They will require hard work and some sacrifice, but something can be done!

As my friend John Perkins likes to say, "We cannot just look at our communities as communities of needs, but also as communities of assets." God has provided more than enough resources and gifted us with enough wisdom and expertise to meet all the world's needs. Our choice is between becoming overwhelmed with the challenges and cursing the darkness, or going on a treasure hunt to find what God has placed at our disposal to bring holistic transformation to lives and communities.

I remember sitting on a church platform, preparing to speak, when the pastor approached the podium. I thought he was about to introduce me, but first he made a startling announcement.

"After much prayer, my wife and I have decided to resign from pastoring this church."

My jaw dropped. The congregation sat stunned, and I was stunned too.

Who in their right mind would invite a guest speaker (me) on the very day he was going to resign?

After the pastor made his shocking announcement, he sat down. The associate pastor, now at a loss for words, managed to introduce me. To make matters worse, my sermon topic for that Sunday (and I am not making this up) was "Never Quit!"

Following the service, I joined the pastor and his wife for lunch. I inquired as delicately as possible about his reasons for resigning the church. His answer was simple: "There are just too many problems in this church and community." I tried to be sympathetic, but I couldn't help but think that what this pastor saw as problems, God saw as opportunities.

When former congressman Tony Hall met Mother Teresa, he asked her, "How can we hope to solve the problems of the hungry, the sick, the poor, and the oppressed since there is such an overwhelming number of them?"

Her reply was simply, "You do the thing that's in front of you."[2]

From the very beginning, working to help the poor has always been part of the work of the church. Believers in the early church were marked not only by the *passion* of their faith (a passion so strong that it sometimes led to persecution and even martyrdom) but also by the *compassion* of their hearts. Will Durant, a historian not always sympathetic toward Christianity, could not help but remark on the good works the early church performed on behalf of the needy.

> Never had the world seen such a dispensation of alms as was now organized by the church...She helped widows and orphans, the sick and the infirm, prisoners, victims of natural catastrophes; and she frequently intervened to protect the lower orders from unusual exploitation or excessive taxation. In many cases priests, on attaining their episcopacy, gave all their property to the poor...Basil established a famous hospital and the first asylum for lepers...Widows were enlisted to distribute charity, and found in this work a new significance for their lonely lives.[3]

Such compassionate acts of service can be found throughout the pages of church history. This thread runs through every generation of the church. A little closer to our own time, William Wilberforce worked to abolish the slave trade, Martin Luther King drew on a biblical vision of equality to challenge racist laws in America, and Mother Teresa gave her life to the work of comforting the dying. These examples don't even begin to exhaust the countless examples of courageous Christians making a difference. And sometimes a whole movement for change can begin with the commitment of one solitary individual who is committed to following Jesus' example.

Declaration 4

> *Compassion revolutionaries change their priorities so more time and resources can flow to others. They don't allow self-interest to completely determine their decisions and votes, but consider how their choices affect the poor and needy.*

Somehow, regardless of how busy we are or how limited our resources might seem, we always find time to do the things that are most important to us. We make sacrifices, change our schedules, and muster our failing strength to do the things we really care about. Becoming a compassion revolutionary requires a reorientation of our hearts and minds so that helping others becomes a priority. And it requires recapturing the biblical vision of the Christian life as a life of service. If we can't think beyond our own wants and needs, we'll never be able to really embrace the needs of others. It starts with an act of repentance—choosing not to be consumed with ourselves and instead to be moved with the needs of others. We follow Jesus' example of being a servant.

In an excellent article called "Welcoming Interruptions," George O. Wood reminds us that "showing compassion almost always involves interruption and inconvenience." He points out that Jesus performed most of His miracles while on the way to do something else. For example, in Mark 5, Jesus is interrupted by Jairus, the ruler of a local synagogue, whose 12-year-old daughter is dying. Jesus leaves off the ministry He is presently involved in and begins the journey to Jairus' home. But on the way, He is interrupted again when a woman with a bleeding condition presses through the crowd so that she might touch the hem of His garment.

> What did Jesus do? Did He say, "I've got more important things to do. I've already detoured because a 12-year-old girl is dying. I don't have time for you."
>
> Oh, no! Jesus stopped, turned around and told the woman that strength had gone out of Him. She was healed.

Why did Jesus let Himself be interrupted? Because He had compassion on those who suffered. When He said the "strength went out from Him," He was declaring a truth that describes what happens in all who help others. It takes something out of you! Compassion will cost you time, effort, strength, and money.

But it's worth it! Oh, yes! When we touch another with compassion, it makes all the difference in the world.[4]

We need to make compassion such a priority in our lives that we allow ourselves to be interrupted by need, just as Jesus did. And as with anything we make a priority, we'll find the time and resources to do the things that we truly think are important.

In addition to our time and money, another resource we have is our vote. We need to take responsibility to vote with hearts of compassion and not merely in our own self-interest. We should show our caring by our support for the kinds of public policies that make a difference. Sometimes institutions and policies are unjust or are designed to help the rich at the expense of the poor. As we fill out our ballots, we need to ask ourselves how "the least of these" are likely to be affected by a yes or no vote. Sometimes people are poor because of their sins. But very often people are poor because of *our* sins—sins of gluttony, greed, and thinking primarily of ourselves.

As compassion revolutionaries, we will challenge unjust and unfair laws and policies. Martin Luther King Jr. reminds us that being a Good Samaritan is more than just meeting an immediate need. It includes changing situations that are unfair and unjust.

> We are called to play the Good Samaritan on life's roadside…but one day we must come to see that the whole Jericho road must be transformed so that men and women will not be constantly beaten and robbed. True compassion is more than flinging a coin to a beggar. It comes to see that a system that produces beggars needs to be repaved. We are called to be the Good Samaritan, but after you lift so many people out of the ditch you start to ask, maybe the whole road to Jericho needs to be repaved.[5]

Declaration 5

Compassion revolutionaries reach out to meet needs worldwide without neglecting the needs in their own backyard.

Following one of our Convoy of Hope outreaches, one church discovered that human need and the opportunity to show compassion were literally in its own backyard.

A young woman and her daughter met me as they were leaving an outreach in a major urban area here in the United States. The little girl was so sweet. She beamed as she raised up a balloon in one hand and a candy cane in the other. Her giddy smile reminded me of Christmas!

"We've never been treated with such kindness," the mother said, putting her arm around her daughter.

"Do you live in this area?" I asked. I wanted to be sure someone could follow up later with further help.

"We live over there," the woman said. They both pointed in the direction of a neighborhood close by.

"In the neighborhood behind the church?"

"Well, not exactly," she answered cautiously. She thought a moment. "May I show you?"

She led me through a few streets in the direction of the church. Then we went around behind it, where I saw an overflowing Dumpster and an old broken-down church bus.

As we approached the Dumpster, the little girl pointed. "There," she said innocently. "We live there."

My heart collapsed when I looked behind the Dumpster and saw a makeshift shelter of plywood and cardboard.

I was incredulous. "You live here?"

They both nodded.

The church, which had participated in the outreach, had not even noticed the need that was literally in its own backyard. It was quite a wake-up call. The parishioners realized that they were going through the religious motions, but the compassion of Jesus was missing in action.

Churches in America have responded with great compassion to such worldwide horrors as famine, tsunamis, the AIDS/HIV epidemic, and the millions of orphans left in the wake of these catastrophes. Yet many have found it easier to show compassion across the seas than across the street. Shane Claiborne challenges us, "Tithes, tax-exempt donations, and short-term mission trips, while they accomplish some good, can also function as outlets that allow us to appease our consciences and still remain a safe distance from the poor."[6]

For Jesus, outreach begins nearby. In Acts 1:8, He promises to send His Spirit to empower His disciples so they can be His witnesses "in Jerusalem, and in all Judea and Samaria, and to the ends of the earth." Concentric circles of ministry progress from the nearby to the faraway.

In 1979, Mother Teresa was presented with the Nobel Peace Prize. During a Who's Who banquet to honor her lifetime of achievement, she appeared wearing a simple Indian sari, more suited for a peasant than a prizewinner. In her gentle, somewhat feeble voice, she challenged the guests to "find the poor here, right in your own home, first, and then begin to love there, and find out about your next-door neighbor—do you know who they are?"

Declaration 6

Compassion revolutionaries look for ways to cooperate with others to bring about healing and change.

Jesus said that the way we love one another is the surest sign to the world that we are His disciples. How are we to expect people to believe our words about a gospel of love and grace if we show little of those things to each other?

Near the end of a flight in Ireland, I gazed out the window of my plane, expecting to see the fabled stone walls between the farms. But from my vantage point, I couldn't see any walls. Curious, I asked an Irishman sitting nearby what had happened to the stone walls I had heard so much about.

"Oh," he said, "the walls are down there, but you can't see them right now because it's harvest time and the crops are high."

What a great picture of how we can remain distinct while working together for the same end. We need to fix our eyes on the ripe harvest and not on the geographic, ethnic, economic, and denominational walls that separate us.

Theology and religious practices are not the only things that divide us. We need to be aware of the great danger of turning compassion issues into partisan political issues. How sad if the needs of the impoverished become a political football and we fumble our attempts to make a difference because we resist getting involved in issues that seem to belong to the other party.

Conservatives and progressives may disagree about a lot of things, but that doesn't mean they can't work together on the critical challenges that face us in the compassion revolution. In my work with faith-based initiatives, I had the joy of seeing some pretty fierce political opponents working hand in hand on compassion issues. I wish I could have seen it more often. In a time of strong partisanship, maybe these very issues could begin to bring our country together again. Wouldn't you love to see Democrats, Republicans, and Independents all working with each other to bring hope to the hopeless and help to the helpless?

We can accomplish so much more when we work together than we can when we work by ourselves. Our ability to make a major difference is multiplied by cooperation. Therefore, we cannot allow our doctrinal or political disagreements and our pride to get in the way of making common cause in defense of the poor.

Declaration 7

> *Compassion revolutionaries find the joy and fulfillment that comes from making a difference in other people's lives.*

Although serving the poor can be a lot of work, I can tell you personally that the end result is a tremendous experience of joy and satisfaction. If you are still not sure, why not try a little experiment? Give a little of your time. Give a little of your money. See how it feels. I can guarantee you that the result will be a desire to get even more involved. Changing lives is life-changing!

We've explored many avenues for involvement throughout this book—many ways you can get personally involved in the compassion revolution. In addition to the money you can allocate to help meet the desperate needs of the poor in our nation and throughout the world, you might consider one of the many practical ways you can personally make a difference. Perhaps you could spend a couple of hours a week at the local food bank or volunteer at the hospital. You could donate blood or be part of the Big Brother Big Sister program in your community. Maybe you could become a volunteer firefighter or sign up for a charity run. You could participate in one of our Convoy of Hope outreaches. Local shelters always need clothing, and care facilities need people to spend time with the elderly. The opportunities are many. The need is for people who want to make a difference by getting involved. Could it be time for you to explore your place in the compassion revolution?

Vernon Grounds tells the story of a woman who dreamed that she was having a conversation with God. She was angry about all the suffering and evil she saw around her, so she complained to the Lord. "Why don't You do something about all this?"

"I did," God gently replied. "I created you."

Conclusion:

AN EXTRAORDINARY LIFE

When I think about the immensity of the task set before those of us who have chosen to be compassion revolutionaries, I consider the story of Jesus feeding the five thousand. A large crowd gathers to hear Jesus teach. The day wears on, and being a person of deep compassion, Jesus becomes concerned that the crowd has gone too long without any food. He has been meeting their spiritual hunger, but He wants to meet their physical hunger as well. He tells His disciples to give the people something to eat.

The disciples are confused and probably just a little frustrated with Jesus. Why can't He be more realistic? They don't even have enough food to feed their own small group, much less a large crowd. Nor do they have enough money to go buy food for the hungry masses. With their meager resources, they couldn't possibly meet Jesus' request.

At moments like these, Jesus turns addition into multiplication.

All the disciples could dig up was the ordinary lunch of an ordinary boy—five barley loaves and two fish. The boy agreed to offer what he had, and Jesus multiplied it. What would have been just an ordinary lunch became an extraordinary lunch. Jesus took this small offering and used it to feed five thousand people. The smallest seed was turned into an overflowing harvest. When everyone had eaten, there was more food left over than they had started with! God seems to enjoy making a lot out of very little (see Proverbs 3:9-10; 19:17; Malachi 3:10; Matthew 13:1-23; Luke 6:38).

This story begs us to ask ourselves, are we satisfied with living ordinary lives—holding tightly to everything we have, keeping it all, playing it safe? Or do we yearn for extraordinary lives? For the adventure of giving it all away to Jesus and watching Him multiply our lives to touch the multitudes with compassion?

En route to my office in Washington DC, I usually travel past Arlington National Cemetery. There among the rolling hills are thousands of white marble headstones that commemorate the brave men and women who gave their lives defending the freedoms we all enjoy. From time to time I like to visit the graves of these soldiers and note when they were born and when they died. The names and dates are different, but each of these grave markers has one thing in common.

All these epitaphs have a dash between the date the people were born and the date they died. That seemingly insignificant little dash represents those people's lives. They were born on a certain date, and they died on a certain date, often in sacrificial service of the country they loved. But their lives were lived out in all the years between the dates.

You too have been blessed with a dash called life. You might be at the beginning, in the middle, or near the end of your dash, but the question is, how will you use what is left? Once your final date is inscribed on the right side of the dash, what will you have accomplished for Jesus? What difference will your life have made? Will you leave the world a better place than it was when you entered it? Will you have lived for yourself, or will you have given yourself for others? Mother Teresa reminds us, "At the end of life we will not be judged by how many diplomas we have received, how much money we have made, how many great things we have done. We will be judged by, 'I was hungry and you gave me to eat, I was naked and you clothed me, I was homeless and you took me in.'"

You were not created to live an ordinary existence. God has something more for you—a life of experiencing the joy and adventure of making a difference in other people's lives. An extraordinary God placed you on this planet to accomplish extraordinary things. So heed the call and join the compassion revolution! Even if you only have limited resources and gifts— just some bread and fish—God can do something amazing with your life!

WHAT THE BIBLE SAYS ABOUT POVERTY AND THE POOR

W e've looked at a number of Bible verses in the course of this book that point toward God's perspective on poverty, economic injustice, and the poor. In this appendix, we'll take a quick tour of a few of the more than 2000 verses in the Bible that refer to this topic. It is a major theme throughout the Scriptures, not just isolated in a place here and there. As a matter of fact, it is the second-most common theme in the Old Testament. Only the topic of idolatry is addressed more frequently than poverty! So let's begin our brief survey in the Old Testament.

From the very beginning of time, people have become the victims of poverty due to physical inability (sickness, age, or disability), natural disasters (famines, fires, or floods), or the oppression of those who took advantage of them. Poverty has always been a part of living in a fallen world, a world that has neglected God's path and sought its own.

No Poor Among You

When God made a covenant to have an intimate relationship with the Israelites, His chosen people, He gave them laws to help them live holy, healthy, and just lives. One of the issues that received a lot of attention in the Mosaic law was the importance of caring for the poor and underprivileged. God wanted His people to be different from the cultures around them, societies that neglected the impoverished or blamed them for their difficult state. He also wanted His people to be different from those who thought that the only good use of people from other countries was to make them slaves.

The law of Moses emphasized the need for compassion. God expected His people to show concern for one another. Leviticus 25:35-36 summarizes this perspective and emphasizes our responsibility to care for one another.

> If one of your countrymen becomes poor and is unable to support himself among you, help him as you would an alien or a temporary resident, so he can continue to live among you. Do not take interest of any kind from him, but fear your God, so that your countryman may continue to live among you.

Care for the poor was to be a priority for God's people—looking out for those who, because of their disadvantages, could not look out for themselves.

One of the ways this is ensured is through the system of gleaning, which gave the underprivileged access to farmers' extra produce. This system helped prevent starvation and malnutrition. Leviticus 19:9-10 instructs, "When you reap the harvest of your land, do not reap to the very edges of your field or gather the gleanings of your harvest. Do not go over your vineyard a second time or pick up the grapes that have fallen. Leave them for the poor and the alien. I am the LORD your God."

Gleaning was not a practice of pure charity because the poor had to work to gather the excess of the harvest for themselves. The landowners offered help along with the dignity of work. You'll also see this practice mentioned in the book of Ruth. In fact, I came across a news article about a group of Christian farmers in Oregon who are, even today, practicing this biblical mandate when they harvest their fields.

Deuteronomy 15:4 plainly states God's economic goal for His people: "There should be no poor among you." The accumulation of property could lead to resources being too centralized in a few hands, so God instituted the Year of Jubilee (Leviticus 25:8-43). Under this system, all properties reverted to their original owners every fiftieth year. That meant that no one ever needed to fear permanent destitution. Similarly, Deuteronomy 15:1-2 commands that all debts be cancelled every seven years. Once again, this kept anyone from finding themselves in a state of permanent impoverishment and indebtedness. To us, this seems like a radical economic system and may be problematic to those of us who believe in capitalism. But its purpose was to ensure as much economic justice as possible. With such laws, God interrupted the human systems that create poverty by releasing people from debt, giving freedom to slaves, and redistributing property. This should at least remind us where God's priorities lie. He is more concerned about preventing poverty than He is about ensuring economic growth!

Deuteronomy 15:11 is an excellent summary of how we are to approach the issue of poverty. "There will always be poor people in the land. Therefore I command you to be openhanded toward your brothers and toward the poor and needy in your land."

Seek Justice for the Poor

Those who are tempted to neglect the poor or take advantage of them should remember that God is the protector of those who cannot protect themselves, the provider for those who cannot provide for themselves, the one who fights for those who cannot fight for themselves. As the psalmist reminds us, "The LORD secures justice for the poor and upholds the cause of the needy" (Psalm 140:12). And He expects us to do the same: "Defend the cause of the weak and fatherless; maintain the rights of the poor and oppressed. Rescue the weak and needy; deliver them from the hand of the wicked" (Psalm 82:3-4). Those who oppress the poor will receive judgment. In the midst of a chapter full of judgments on those who practice all kinds of sin, we find this imprecation: "Cursed is the man who withholds justice from the alien, the fatherless or the widow" (Deuteronomy 27:19). As we shall see in a moment, this concern for justice was one of the most common themes of the Old Testament prophets.

But first, let's take a quick stop at the book of Proverbs. This collection of bite-size pieces of wisdom has a lot to say about how we are to treat the poor, pointing especially to the blessings given to those who make this a priority. Here is a sampling of some of the proverbs dealing with poverty:

- "A generous man will prosper; he who refreshes others will himself be refreshed" (11:25).

- "He who oppresses the poor shows contempt for their Maker, but whoever is kind to the needy honors God" (14:31).

- "He who is kind to the poor lends to the LORD, and he will reward him for what he has done" (19:17).

- "If a man shuts his ear to the cry of the poor, he too will cry out and not be answered" (21:13).

- "A generous man will himself be blessed, for he shares his food with the poor" (22:9).

- "He who gives to the poor will lack nothing, but he who closes his eyes to them receives many curses" (28:27).

- "The righteous care about justice for the poor, but the wicked have no such concern" (29:7).

- "Speak up for those who cannot speak for themselves, for the rights of all who are destitute. Speak up and judge fairly; defend the rights of the poor and needy" (31:8-9).

- "[A wife of noble character] opens her arms to the poor and extends her hands to the needy" (31:20).

Set Apart to Serve

In the prophetic books of the Old Testament, the prophets consistently admonish the people against injustice and neglect of the poor. Their voices sound like thunder, and they mince no words describing God's feelings both about the plight of the poor and about those who take advantage of them or neglect them. Some of the most passionate words of Scripture are spoken on behalf of the poor and needy.

Isaiah raises his voice to proclaim the need for change and repentance: "Wash and make yourselves clean. Take your evil deeds out of my sight! Stop doing wrong, learn to do right! Seek justice, encourage the oppressed. Defend the cause of the fatherless, plead the case of the widow" (Isaiah 1:16-17). And then, later in the same book, "Is this not the kind of fasting I have chosen: to loose the chains of injustice and untie the cords of the yoke, to set the oppressed free and break every yoke? Is it not to share your food with the hungry and provide the poor wanderer with shelter—when you see the naked, to clothe him, and not to turn away from your own flesh and blood?" (Isaiah 58:6-7). To those who respond to this message with appropriate action, God promises, "Your light will rise in the darkness, and your night will become like the noonday. The LORD will guide you always; he will satisfy your needs in a sun-scorched land" (Isaiah 58:10-11). This promise points to one of the themes of the compassionate revolution—that God's blessings and great joy come to people who don't live their lives for themselves alone, but instead reach out to others.

God calls His people to be different from those around them who neglect the poor. Ezekiel 16:49 describes one of Israel's neighbors: "Now this was the sin of your sister Sodom: She and her daughters were arrogant, overfed and unconcerned; they did not help the poor and needy." But Jeremiah says that God's people were no better:

> They are fat, they are sleek,
> They also excel in deeds of wickedness;
> They do not plead the cause,
> The cause of the orphan, that they may prosper;
> And they do not defend the rights of the poor
>   (Jeremiah 5:28 NASB).

Very few of the Old Testament prophets did not in some way address this issue, which was so close to God's heart—the justice and mercy we should show in our actions toward people in need. We'll end our quick survey of the Old Testament with these words of the prophet Zechariah: "This is what the LORD Almighty says, 'Administer true justice; show mercy and compassion to one another. Do not oppress the widow or the fatherless, the alien or the poor'" (Zechariah 7:9-10).

Jesus' Mission Statement

In the New Testament, we find this same theme frequently showing up in the Gospel records of Jesus' life and teaching. His compassion for the poor was a key element of the mission statement that He announced at the very beginning of His ministry:

> The Spirit of the Lord is on me,
>   because he has anointed me
>   to preach good news to the poor.
> He has sent me to proclaim freedom for the prisoners
>   and recovery of sight for the blind,
> to release the oppressed,
>   to proclaim the year of the Lord's favor (Luke 4:18-19).

If we, Jesus' disciples, are to follow in His footsteps of compassion, we must listen to His call for a radically different way of thinking about our possessions so they don't possess us. Instead of hoarding our wealth, Jesus challenges us to give it to those who need it most: "Sell your possessions and give to the poor. Provide purses for yourselves that will not wear out, a treasure in heaven that will not be exhausted, where no thief comes near and no moth destroys. For where your treasure is, there your heart will be also" (Luke 12:33-34). We will never give abundantly as long as we hold tight to our possessions and make an idol of our financial security.

Jesus calls His disciples—including us—to begin thinking differently about the poor and about what really matters in our own lives. "Then Jesus said to his host, 'When you give a luncheon or dinner, do not invite your friends, your brothers or relatives, or your rich neighbors; if you do, they may invite you back and so you will be repaid. But when you give a banquet, invite the poor, the crippled, the lame, the blind, and you will be blessed. Although they cannot repay you, you will be repaid at the resurrection of the righteous'" (Luke 14:12-14).

No Excuses

Some Christians have wrongly interpreted Jesus' statement in John 12:8, "You will always have the poor among you," to mean that issues like poverty and injustice should be of less significance for believers than the supposedly more important spiritual matters. When taken in the context of all Jesus had to say about the poor, this obviously cannot be the correct way to understand this verse. As a matter of fact, Jesus' hearers would have recognized this as a quotation from Deuteronomy 15:11. They would also have known the rest of the verse: "Therefore I command you to be openhanded toward your brothers and toward the poor and needy in your land." Jesus may have been pointing to a sad reality, but it was a reality He wanted His hearers to do something about!

Of course, Jesus gave one of His strongest statements about how Christians should treat the poor in His parable of the sheep and the goats.

> Then the King will say to those on His right, "Come, you who are blessed of My Father, inherit the kingdom prepared for you from the foundation of the world. For I was hungry, and you gave Me something to eat; I was thirsty, and you gave Me something to drink; I was a stranger, and you invited Me in; naked, and you clothed Me; I was sick, and you visited Me; I was in prison, and you came to Me."
>
> Then the righteous will answer Him, saying, "Lord, when did we see You hungry, and feed You, or thirsty, and give You something

to drink? And when did we see You a stranger, and invite You in, or naked, and clothe You? When did we see You sick, or in prison, and come to You?"

The King will answer and say to them, "Truly I say to you, to the extent that you did it to one of these brothers of Mine, even the least of them, you did it to Me" (Matthew 25:34-46 NASB).

In other words, we determine whether we are sheep or goats by the way we help the poor. These are sobering words indeed, and an even more sobering thought follows—if we neglect the least of these, we are neglecting Jesus Himself! As Mother Teresa reminds us, "In the poor we meet Jesus in His most distressing disguises." This passage tells us that we see the very face of Jesus in the face of the poor, and if we want to serve Jesus, we must serve the poor.

The joy of serving the poor.

Radical Giving

The apostle Paul continues Jesus' emphasis but with more direct teaching on the act of giving. He quotes a saying of Jesus that is not contained in the

Gospels but rings with the truth of a statement from the Lord Himself: "It is more blessed to give than to receive" (Acts 20:35). Giving was part of the lifeblood of the early church. Acts 2:44 describes how the early Christians used their money and possessions: "All the believers were together and had everything in common. Selling their possessions and goods, they gave to anyone as he had need."

God gives to us so that we might be able to give to others. Paul teaches a principle of generosity in our giving. He even suggests that giving should be fun! "Remember this: Whoever sows sparingly will also reap sparingly, and whoever sows generously will also reap generously. Every man should give what he has decided in his heart to give, not reluctantly or under compulsion, for God loves a cheerful giver" (2 Corinthians 9:6-7).

The apostle John wonders if people who fail to be generous have experienced God's love in their own hearts. Generosity is one of the marks of the true believer. "If anyone has material possessions and sees his brother in need but has no pity on him, how can the love of God be in him?" (1 John 3:17).

The apostle James's letter is particularly emphatic about the importance of opening our hearts and wallets to the needy. It is part of the definition of true religion: "Religion that God our Father accepts as pure and faultless is this: to look after orphans and widows in their distress and to keep oneself from being polluted by the world" (James 1:27).

As one of the great compassion revolutionaries of all time, James reminds us that feeling sorry for the poor or wishing them well is not enough. We need to put our compassionate feelings into action! "Suppose a brother or sister is without clothes and daily food. If one of you says to him, 'Go, I wish you well; keep warm and well fed,' but does nothing about his physical needs, what good is it? In the same way, faith by itself, if it is not accompanied by action, is dead" (James 2:15-17).

Sounding like one of the Old Testament prophets, James warns of the judgment to come on those who live in comfort while neglecting the needy: "Now listen, you rich people, weep and wail because of the misery that is coming upon you. Your wealth has rotted, and moths have eaten your clothes. Your gold and silver are corroded. Their corrosion will testify against you and eat your flesh like fire. You have hoarded wealth in the last days...You have lived on earth in luxury and self-indulgence. You have fattened yourselves in the day of slaughter" (James 5:1-5). Surely we do not want to be found in that category!

This quick survey of what the Scriptures say about the poor reminds us that this is an overwhelmingly important issue in God's Word. In these few pages, we have only dipped our toes into the subject. Many other passages parallel the ones we have looked at. But these passages clearly reveal that compassion in action is not optional for the believer. It's a fundamental characteristic of the one who wishes to walk in God's path. The evidence of its importance is unquestionable.

FREQUENTLY ASKED QUESTIONS ABOUT FOSTER CARE AND ADOPTION

Foster Care

1. What is foster parenting? Being a foster parent means providing a safe, loving, and nurturing temporary home for children in the foster care system. As a foster parent, you will be assigned a qualified caseworker to serve alongside you to assure the well-being of your family and the foster child.

2. What are the children in foster care like? For the most part, children in foster care are just like other kids except that, in some cases, they may have special needs due to neglect and abandonment. They range in age from infants to teenagers. Children in foster care come from varied backgrounds and different family situations, but all are in foster care because their parents are unable to care for them for some reason.

3. How long will the children stay in foster care? A large percentage of the children will eventually return home to their birth parents. When the children are not able to reunite with their birth parents, adoption by the foster family or another family becomes the goal.

4. What does it take to become a foster parent? Most foster care agencies offer orientations to help you determine if foster care is right for you. These usually include several weeks of training that provide the tools you need to be a great foster parent. In general, you can be a foster parent if you are in good health and at least 21 years old. You can be married or single. All adults in your household will be subject to a criminal background check by your state's central registry for abuse and neglect. The application process includes proof of income and a home that is free from health and safety hazards and large enough to comfortably accommodate a child. Once you are cleared by the state, your caseworker will schedule a time to do a "home study" to make sure your home meets the state's requirements.

5. *What kind of financial support is available to help me care for the child?* Every month, you will receive a check to cover the costs of raising a child. This includes additional funds for clothing and, in the case of infants, diapers. Medicaid covers the children's medical expenses.

6. *Will I be required to relate to the foster child's birth parents?* The birth parents are allowed monthly visits with their child. These visits are arranged by the caseworker and usually take place at a neutral location.

7. *What kind of ongoing support will I receive from the agency?* Your caseworker will work alongside you throughout the child's stay in your home. Depending on the agency you choose, you may have opportunities to attend special training sessions throughout the year. Day care, counseling and therapy, and summer camp may be available. Joining a foster parent support group is a good way to get advice and assistance from experienced foster parents.

8. *What influence will a foster child have on my biological children?* Becoming a foster family can be a very positive experience for your children by teaching them to make room for others and to share their home and possessions. It can temper their tendency toward materialism as they learn that many other children do not have the privileges and possessions they take for granted.

9. *What if I want to adopt a child from foster care?* Nationwide, a third of all foster children will become available for adoption. Most states do not charge families to adopt a foster child. You can learn more about this in the FAQs on adoption.

10. *What do foster parents do when their foster children decide to return to their biological parents?* This can be very challenging because of the natural bonding that takes place between foster parents and foster children. Parents have to consider that success is based on the quality of the experience they provide for the children rather than the length of time the children are with them. The parents' investment of love, solid biblical values, and positive personal skills will stay with the children for the remainder of their lives. In addition, most foster children remain close to their foster parents even after returning to their biological families.

Adoption

(The following information is from Focus on the Family and used by permission.)

1. Are all adoptions really expensive? Cost can be a major factor for many adoptions, but it can vary. International and private adoptions tend to cost more due to lawyer and agency fees and usually range between $15,000 and $40,000. However, not all adoptions are this expensive. In many states, adoption through the foster care system is less than $500. Regardless of which type of adoption you pursue, the U.S. government provides up to $10,000 in tax credit for each adopted child.

2. How long does an adoption take? Most domestic adoptions take between one and two years. International adoptions and special cases can take longer.

3. Will the government always be watching over my shoulder? The state government's role in adoption is to help ensure that a child is placed in a loving home that is a good match for both the parents and the child. A family looking to adopt must complete a background check, training, and a home study to determine if they are able to provide a safe environment for additional children (this is true with international adoption as well). After a child is placed in the home, the government will continue to check in on the family and write a post-placement report for the court. However, once the adoption is finalized, the government has no involvement in how you parent your children. At that point, parental rights are exactly the same as with a biological child.

4. How will an adopted child affect my biological children? A child who has lost one or both parents inevitably experiences trauma. You can't completely protect your family, but gaining knowledge and understanding of the child you're adopting will go a long way. Start investigating the community resources that are available to you and have conversations with your children. Involving them in the process will help them adapt to the coming changes. Often, children already in the home can help other children adjust to the family.

5. Will I love an adopted child as much as a biological child? If you ask adoptive parents this question, they'll probably smile as they remember the same question running through their minds. Many will tell you that the instant they met their child, they could not deny that this child was a part of their family.

6. Can the birth parents come back and take the child? Once the parental rights have been terminated and all appeals have been exhausted, the biological parents cannot take their children back. Many foster parents open their homes to children with the hopes of adoption. In many cases, the biological parents' parental rights have been terminated. However, in certain situations, a family may take in a child with a legal risk that the parental rights may not yet be terminated and the child could be returned to the birth family. However, the family would be aware of this risk before the child was placed in their home. (Special circumstances may apply for Native American children.)

7. Don't all kids who need to be adopted have lots of problems? Most children in foster care have experienced some form of trauma, some while they were still in the womb and others in birth families or foster care families. However, educating yourself on the challenges you will face will better prepare you for the child who is coming into your home. Many times as we begin to dig deeper into the trauma of our adoptive children, issues, fears, and concerns from our own life surface. God often uses our honesty and brokenness to help heal our children.[1]

A PRAYER FOR COMPASSION REVOLUTIONARIES

Heavenly Father,

I come into Your presence, humbly seeking Your will and Your wisdom for the direction of my life. The navigation of my course I give to You, for I am merely the administrator of the assignments. You have walked with me through each trial and tribulation. You have held me up when at my weakest. You have been my rock in a world of sand.

I praise You and You alone, O holy and righteous God.

I have heard that prayer has subdued the strength of fire. It has bridled the rage of lions, hushed anarchy to rest, extinguished wars, appeased the elements, burst the chains of death, expanded the gates of heaven, assuaged diseases, dispelled frauds, rescued cities from destruction, stayed the sun in its course, and arrested the progress of the thunderbolt. In this communion with You, there is an all-sufficient panoply, a treasure undiminished, a mine that is never exhausted, a sky unobscured by clouds, a heaven unruffled by the storm. It is the root, the fountain, the mother of a thousand blessings!

Thus, I know, nothing is impossible for You.

Father, You have opened my eyes to many things, for while I was wallowing in the mud, You saw past the horrific sight, and washed and cleansed me from the core of my being. How lowly I was indeed. I was rejected and without hope. Yet You lifted me up, put a robe around my body, and crowned me as Your child, and today I stand as a new creation in You.

I praise Your name!

Father, as You stretched out Your hand and brought me forth from despair and shame, so teach me to reach out to those the world has passed by. Just as You took my broken body and healed my wounds, give me the compassion to serve the many who are in need. Just as You gave hope to the hopeless, so too grant me strength to bear others' burdens for the cause of Christ, that lives would be saved and communities transformed.

It is easy for me to stay where I am comfortable. Give me the courage of Daniel to go where I know I must—to the place where You have called me. May I follow with vigor and perseverance, that You alone may be glorified by the labor of my hand.

The world is hungry and lost, and it needs to feel the love that You have shown to me. I dare not be silent and look the other way, passing by in fear or in prideful self-concern. May my faith be more than words.

In You, I can say to the mountain to move from here to there, and it will be done. So too, give me faith that the barriers in our culture today will be broken down and lives restored. Forgive us for looking the other direction while thousands die every day. May the Spirit fill us by the multitudes so that this tragedy would not continue.

Where You lead, I will follow. Where Your children are hungry, beaten, and forgotten, there I will be to lift the glass, to carry the food, to serve with every last breath. For this body belongs to You, and for eternity I will sing Your praises for remembering me when I was no different.

May I never forget who I was, and may I never forget what I am called to do.

In the righteous name of the Lord Jesus Christ, I pray.

Amen.

National Day of Prayer Task Force
Chairman, Mrs. Shirley Dobson
Prayer by Mr. John Bornschein
and Mr. John Chrysostom

SOME RECOMMENDED COMPASSION ORGANIZATIONS

The following is a sampling of global Christian compassion organizations that are worth exploring as you consider whom to support financially or through volunteerism. You can learn more about each of them by visiting the website listed after the brief description of each organization. Make sure to do your own homework researching these charities because the quality of an organization and its leadership is subject to change. A couple of watchdog groups can be helpful in your research. Charity Navigator (www.charitynavagator.org) is a leading evaluator of charities based on their financial health and stewardship of resources. Another helpful organization is the Evangelical Council for Financial Accountability (www. ecfa.org), which looks for Christian organizations that meet specific standards.

Spend some time getting to know these partners in the battle against poverty and injustice. These are great resources for every compassion revolutionary.

Bethany Children Services helps families interested in adoption, foster care, and other services that protect and build the quality of life for children.

800-Bethany

bethany.org

Bread for the World seeks justice for the world's hungry by lobbying congress and educating citizens on ways they can participate in serving the poor.
202-639-9400
bread.org

Center for Neighborhood Enterprise works to promote solutions for neighborhoods to reduce crime and violence, restore families, and revitalize low-income communities.
202-518-6500
cneonline.org

The Charity Awards celebrate the outstanding contributions of individuals and organizations that make the world a better place. Philanthropists also are connected to worthy causes and offered ways to leverage their giving.
charityawards.com

Childhelp meets physical, emotional, and spiritual needs of abused, neglected, and at-risk children.
480-922-8212
childhelp.org

Christian Community Development Association serves its membership of community-based organizations through training and networking.
312-733-0200
ccda.org

Compassion International provides poor children with food, shelter, education, and health care.
800-336-7676
compassion.com

Convoy of Hope, Inc. mobilizes people and resources to help the poor through outreaches, disaster response, and ongoing relief and development.
417-823-8998
convoy.org

Evangelicals for Social Action educates the evangelical community on issues such as poverty, reverence for life, and care for creation.
484-384-2990
esa-online.org

Family Research Council promotes marriage and family and the sanctity of human life by effecting government policy.
202-393-2100
frc.org

The Family Center of Gap is a hub of interactive services that offer healing to marriages and families.
717-442-2300
gapfamilycenter.org

FCS Urban Ministries partners with businesses and nonprofits to help bring social, economic, and spiritual rebirth to declining inner-city neighborhoods.
404-627-4304
fcsministries.org

Feed My Starving Children seeks to eliminate starvation by delivering a nutritious food mixture to the poor.
763-504-2919
fmsc.org

Focus on the Family provides education on marriage and parenting and the sanctity of human life.
719-531-5181
focusonthefamily.com

Food for the Hungry serves the poor with food, agriculture, water, and health care.
800-246-6437
fh.org

Habitat for Humanity builds decent and affordable housing for needy families. Home owners invest hundreds of hours of their own labor and make affordable mortgage payments to own the home.
800-422-4828
habitat.org

International Justice Mission is a human rights agency that secures justice for victims of slavery and other forms of violent oppression.
703-465-5495
ijm.org

Joshua Fund sponsors relief projects in Israel and throughout the Middle East.
888-792-4544
joshuafund.net

Leadership Foundation offers expert charitable counsel and innovative giving solutions to donors, churches, and charities.
800-251-4431
serving-leaders.com

Love INC brings churches together across denominational lines to help the poor by meeting immediate needs such as food and clothing, and by offering longer-term programs such as life-skills training and transitional housing.
800-777-5277
loveinc.org

Mercy Corps links professionals to opportunities that alleviate suffering, poverty, and oppression through agriculture, economic development, food and nutrition, women's empowerment, and water and sanitation.
800-292-3355
mercycorps.org

The National Christian Foundation offers expert counsel to help donors give wisely and make an eternal difference with their charitable giving.
800-681-6223
nationalchristian.com

National Day of Prayer Task Force mobilizes the Christian community to pray for America and its leadership in government, military, media, business, education, church, and family.
719-531-3379
ndptf.org

National Hispanic Christian Leadership Conference strives to serve the Hispanic/Latino church by becoming a collective voice for issues such as family, immigration, education, social justice, and poverty.
916-919-7476
nhclc.org

ONE is a grassroots campaign that mobilizes people to fight extreme poverty.
202-495-2700
one.org

Operation Blessing International alleviates human need by offering food, water, and medical services. OBI also responds to victims of disaster by supporting them with emergency supplies.

    757-226-3401

    ob.org

Opportunity International is dedicated to breaking the cycle of poverty by providing small business loans and business services for entrepreneurs who are poor.

    630-242-4100

    opportunity.org

P.E.A.C.E. is a church-based movement to promote reconciliation, plant churches, assist the poor, and educate the next generation of Christians.

    thepeaceplan.com

People for People helps low-income people move from dependency on welfare to sustainability through education, job training, computer training, and counseling.

    215-235-2340

    peopleforpeople.org

Prison Fellowship seeks the transformation of prisoners and their reconciliation to God, family, and community.

    877-478-0100

    prisonfellowship.org

The Salvation Army supports people in need through a wide array of services and programs that meet immediate needs and empower them through teaching life skills.

    (See the website for regional phone numbers.)

    salvationarmyusa.org

Sojourners articulates the biblical call to social justice, inspiring hope and building a movement to transform individuals, communities, the church, and the world. Sojourners works to accomplish this through education, volunteerism, and influencing policy relating to poverty issues.

    202-328-8842

    sojo.net

World Relief empowers local churches to serve the most vulnerable by educating and equipping leaders to build grassroots programs that are sustainable and community driven.

    800-535-5433

    community.wr.org

World Vision is dedicated to working with children, families, and their communities to reach their full potential by tackling the causes of poverty and injustice. World Vision accomplishes this through advocacy, water and sanitation, nutrition and food, and other development services.

888-511-6548

worldvision.org

NOTES

Chapter 2: "Your Dad Is in Heaven": A Convoy of Hope

1. Tony Hall, *Changing the Face of Hunger* (Nashville: W Publishing Group, 2006), 36.

Chapter 3: With

1. Henri Nouwen, Donald McNeil, and Douglas Morrison, *Compassion* (New York: Image Books, 1983), 27.

Chapter 5: Who Are the Poor?

1. Alexandra Cawthorne, "Elderly Poverty: The Challenge Before Us," Center for American Progress, July 30, 2008. www.americanprogress.org/issues/2008/07/elderly_poverty.html.
2. Amy Sherman, *Restorers of Hope* (Eugene, OR: Wipf & Stock, 2007), 45.
3. Sherman, *Restorers of Hope*, 79.
4. Malcolm Gladwell, *The Tipping Point* (New York: Back Bay Books, 2002), 28.

Chapter 6: A Shopping Mall of Compassion

1. Ken Camp, "Second Reformation Will Unify Church, Warren tells Dallas GDOP," Pastors.com, 2005. legacy.pastors.com/RWMT/article.asp?ID=207&ArtID=8280.

Chapter 7: Pro-life for the Poor

1. Kathleen Kingsbury, "The Value of a Human Life: $129,000," Time.com, May 20, 2008. www.time.com/time/health/article/0,8599,1808049,00.html.
2. Rick Warren, *The Purpose-Driven Life* (Grand Rapids: Zondervan, 2002), 23-24.
3. Rich Stearns, *The Hole in Our Gospel* (Nashville: Thomas Nelson, 2009), 238.
4. Rick Warren, *The Purpose-Driven Church* (Grand Rapids: Zondervan, 1995), 145.

Chapter 8: "Is This Heaven?": Caring for Orphans

1. "Child protection from violence, exploitation and abuse," UNICEF, updated July 22, 2009. www.unicef.org/media/media_45451.html.
2. Kirk Noonan, "A Walk for Africa," *Today's Pentecostal Evangel*, July 5, 2009.

Chapter 9: "Please Take My Baby!": Feeding the Hungry

1. Ron Sider, *Rich Christians in an Age of Hunger* (Nashville: Thomas Nelson, 2005), 1.
2. Stearns, *The Hole in Our Gospel*, 134.
3. Jeffrey Sachs, *The End of Poverty* (New York: Penguin, 2006), 1.
4. Stearns, *The Hole in Our Gospel*, 135.

5. Bread for the World. www.bread.org/learn/hunger-basics.

6. Hal Donaldson, "Return to Mathare Valley," *Today's Pentecostal Evangel*, March 4, 2007.

7. Tom Lofton, *Child in the Midst* (Memphis: Main Street Publications, 2008), 8.

Chapter 10: Water Is Life!

1. American Water Works Association. www.drinktap.org/consumerdnn/Default. aspx?tabid=85.

2. *UNICEF Handbook on Water Quality* (New York: UNICEF, 2008).

Chapter 11: "Why Are They Doing This?": Homes for Homeless Families

1. National Alliance to End Homelessness website, July 2009. www.hoopsforthehomeless.org/ docs/hoopspaperfinal.pdf.

2. Alexi Mostrous, "More Families Are Becoming Homeless," *Washington Post*, Sunday, July 12, 2009.

3. Robert Lupton, *Compassion, Justice and the Christian Life* (Ventura: Regal, 2007), 60.

Chapter 12: "Dad, Let's Bring Up the Beds": Foster Care and Adoption

1. From a sermon by Edward Tamminga. www.bethany.org/A55798/bethanyWWW.nsf/c79ed bd86c517a1d852569c800702556/c5ef7ec3ee98fd4f85256f56004d4589?OpenDocument

2. Bob and Cheryl Reccord, *Launching Your Kids for Life* (Nashville: Thomas Nelson, 2005), 32-35.

3. www.terrymeeuwsen.com/biography/family.asp.

Chapter 13: "Today Is a Good Day": Reaching Out to the Cities

1. www.bread.org/learn/us-hunger-issues/poverty-in-america.html.

2. Lupton, *Compassion, Justice, and the Christian Life*, 119.

3. Lupton, *Compassion, Justice, and the Christian Life*, 90.

Chapter 14: Corporate Citizenship

1. Os Hillman, "Faith and Work Facts and Quotes," International Coalition of Workplace Ministries. www.icwm.net/pages.asp?pageid=203.

2. "Interview with CEO of the Original HoneyBaked Ham Company of Georgia, Chuck Bengochea," *Today's Pentecostal Evangel,* July 5, 2009, 27. Used by permission.

3. Eric Riddleberger and Jeff Hittner, "Corporate Social Responsibility," Forbes.com, July 1, 2009.

4. *Past. Present. Future: The 25th Anniversary of Cause Marketing* (Boston: Cone, 2008). www. volunteermatch.org/corporations/resources/cone_research.pdf.

5. "The Benefits of Volunteer Programs: A 2009 Summary Report," Junior Achievement. www. ja.org/files/BenefitsofEmployeeVolunteerPrograms.pdf.

Chapter 15: Miracles of Compassion

1. Shane Claiborne, *The Irresistible Revolution* (Grand Rapids: Zondervan, 2006), 86.

Chapter 16: Revolutionary Giving

1. Sider, *Rich Christians in an Age of Hunger*, 230.
2. Sider, *Rich Christians in an Age of Hunger*, xiv.

Chapter 17: Responsible Compassion

1. Lupton, *Compassion, Justice, and the Christian Life*, 13.
2. Sherman, *Restorers of Hope*, 139.
3. Sider, *Rich Christians in an Age of Hunger*, xv.
4. Marvin Olasky, *Renewing American Compassion* (New York: Simon & Schuster, 1996), 16.
5. Lupton, *Compassion, Justice, and the Christian Life*, 44.

Chapter 18: Avoiding Compassion Fatigue

1. Marvin Olasky, *The Tragedy of American Compassion* (Wheaton: Crossway Books, 2008), 4.
2. Lupton, *Compassion, Justice and the Christian Life*, 72.

Chapter 20: A Declaration of Compassion

1. Stearns, *The Hole in Our Gospel*, 2.
2. Hall, *Changing the Face of Hunger*, 13.
3. Will Durant, *The Age of Faith* (New York: MJF Books, 1997), 78.
4. George O. Wood, "Welcoming Interruptions," *Today's Pentecostal Evangel*, July 5, 2009, 3.
5. Martin Luther King Jr., "A Time to Break the Silence," a sermon delivered at Riverside Church, New York, on April 4, 1967.
6. Claiborne, *Irresistible Revolution*, 157.

Appendix 2: Frequently Asked Questions About Foster Care and Adoption

1. The FAQs on adoption are based on those from the Focus on the Family website and used by permission. www.icareaboutorphans.org/FaqonAdoption.aspx.

To learn more about other Harvest House books
or to read sample chapters, log on to our website:

www.harvesthousepublishers.com

HARVEST HOUSE PUBLISHERS

EUGENE, OREGON